MASTERS AT WORK

MASTERS AT WORK

BECOMING A HAIRSTYLIST

KATE BOLICK

Simon & Schuster
1230 Avenue of the Americas
New York, NY 10020

First Simon & Schuster hardcover edition April 2019

SIMON & SCHUSTER and colophon are registered trademarks
of Simon & Schuster, Inc.

For information about special discounts for bulk purchases,
please contact Simon & Schuster Special Sales at 1-866-506-1949
or business@simonandschuster.com.

The Simon & Schuster Speakers Bureau can bring authors to your
live event. For more information, or to book an event, contact the
Simon & Schuster Speakers Bureau at 1-866-248-3049
or visit our website at www.simonspeakers.com.

Illustrations by Donna Mehalko

Manufactured in the United States of America

1   3   5   7   9   10   8   6   4   2

Library of Congress Cataloging-in-Publication Data

Names: Bolick, Kate, author.
Title: Becoming a hairstylist / Kate Bolick.
Description: First Simon & Schuster hardcover edition. | New York : Simon &
Schuster, 2019. | Series: Masters at work.
Identifiers: LCCN 2018055484 (print) | LCCN 2018056430 (ebook) |
ISBN 9781982115913 (ebook) | ISBN 9781982115906 (hardback)
Subjects: LCSH: LeMoine, Gwenn. | Beauty operators—United States—
Biography. | Hairdressing—Vocational guidance. | BISAC: BUSINESS &
ECONOMICS / Careers / General. | SELF-HELP / Personal Growth /
Success. | EDUCATION / Counseling / Vocational Guidance.
Classification: LCC TT955.L46 (ebook) | LCC TT955.L46 B65 2019 (print) |
DDC 646.7/24092 B—dc23
LC record available at http://lccn.loc.gov/2018055484

ISBN 978-1-9821-1590-6
ISBN 978-1-9821-1591-3 (ebook)

To my fellow members of the Long Brown Hair Band—
Ali, Sophie, and Annie

CONTENTS

1

It is a brutally hot summer afternoon in Manhattan, the kind where merely waiting for the subway causes sweat to drip down your face and drop onto your shirt. If you make the mistake of boarding a car with broken air-conditioning, you're doomed. But when you get out at your stop in the East Village, things start looking up. Walking east on the shady side of Seventh Street, alongside the leafy green of Tompkins Square Park, you turn south onto Avenue B, and know that all is about to be right with the world.

Sure, the block is on the gritty side—but that's a good thing. It's one of the last reminders of the "old" East Village of the 1960s and '70s, when America's punk rock scene and the Nuyorican literary movement were born here. The neighborhood has cleaned up a lot since then, along with so much of New York City.

At first glance, it would appear that your destination, the popular Parlor hair salon, bears no relation to that former countercultural moment. Tucked between a specialty spice shop and an anonymous-looking youth center, Parlor's white-brick facade and black-and-white-striped awnings appear particularly crisp, even jaunty. On the sidewalk out front, a sandwich board with the salon's logo—a whimsical silhouette of a woman with an elegant updo, set into an oval like a Victorian cameo—announces a special on blowouts.

But when you pull open the big plate-glass door, you step into a world where anti-establishment values are paramount. Unlike those other high-end boutique hair salons, the ones that cultivate a glossy, high-fashion veneer—and in a city like New York can feed on all-too-human insecurities—Parlor is a haven of individuality, inclusivity, and comfort. It is easy to understand why so many people celebrated for their idiosyncrasies have been drawn here over the years, from famous actresses such as Molly Ringwald, Mary-Louise Parker, and Rue McClanahan, to the singer-songwriter Adele and the artist William Wegman.

Yes, there's the immediately blissful cool of air-conditioning. But in the grand scheme that's a minor detail. What makes Parlor special is how all the elements, big and small, add up to a uniquely welcoming environment.

Eason Polk, the young man helming the reception desk, welcomes you with a big smile and gestures toward a small table set with two glass jugs: cold water and iced herbal tea.

You help yourself to a glass of each. Originally from Houston, Texas, Eason has worked at Parlor for just over a year as the guest case manager, part of the "front of house" team that wears many hats. Like many of Parlor's employees, when he's not on the clock he devotes his time to creative and volunteer pursuits, in his case designing a high-end clothing line and mentoring LGBTQ youth.

Behind him, in the main room of the salon, the rest of Parlor's beauty squad is occupied in various stages of consulting, cutting, coloring, and styling. The space is bright and cozy at once, sunlight spilling through tall windows onto redbrick walls and dark wood floors. In the background, an upbeat-yet-mellow song by a slightly obscure band is playing. There are seven stations in all, three along each wall and one in the middle. At each is an upholstered green leather swivel chair, like an old barbershop chair, and a giant Art Deco mirror, giving a feminine touch to an otherwise neutral space. Each station is neatly stocked with every conceivable styling tool: multiple types of steel scissors, both the basic "haircutting shears" and the specialized "texturizing shears" for chunking, thinning, and blending. Then there are straight razors, clippers, edgers, sectioning clips, and four types of combs (wide-tooth, tail, barber, and all-purpose, both rubber- and steel-tipped).

The cheerful chatter. The hum of blow-dryers. The friendly music. The ringing phone. The combined effect is like the gentle burbling of a brook, or the low murmur of a fine-dining establishment, without the clatter of cutlery against dishes. Through the back windows you spy a stone Shiva set atop a garden wall, amid a colorful tumble of flowers and plants.

That's when you spot Gwenn LeMoine, standing at her station near the window, talking with a client. Unsurprisingly, given that she created this small universe, her look embodies Parlor's ideals. Not long ago, she uploaded a jokey post to Instagram comparing herself to Sex Pistols frontman Johnny Rotten. On the left is a photograph of Rotten, circa 1970s, age twenty-ish, with his signature snarl and flame-orange hair sticking up all over his head, like an angry baby duck's. On the right is an iPhone picture of LeMoine, year 2018, age fifty-five, with her signature warm smile, thick black eyeglasses framing kind blue eyes, and dyed-red hair cut into a neo-punk shag, with short layers on top and feathery wisps sweeping the back of her neck. "Who does/did it better?" reads the caption. ("I love it!! Looking more like Johnny's fav designer Vivienne Westwood!" writes one commenter.)

On this sweltering day, LeMoine is in a midlength sleeveless black jersey dress with a handkerchief hem and black Doc Marten brogues. Her copper hair gleams prettily in the sun, like a shiny penny.

Her client is in her late fifties, thick chin-length curls dyed a dark chestnut brown, nearly black. She is at an impasse.

"I'm just sick of the upkeep," she says to LeMoine. "But at the same time, I'm not sure I'm ready to go totally gray."

LeMoine nods. She gets it.

"Strangely enough," the client adds, "it's my husband who keeps encouraging me to go gray. But my women friends disagree. They think I should keep my hair the way it is. I don't know why."

LeMoine nods again. "Maybe hanging out with a gray-haired friend will make them feel older," she ventures. "Or, maybe it will make them feel pressured to go gray themselves."

As they continue to muse over the social implications of going gray, LeMoine pulls out her iPhone and calls up an image bank of gray-hair options. Scrolling through, she explains that there are ways to color the hair that show a lot of the gray, but not all of it, and require less maintenance.

The client asks questions. Their conversation becomes so absorbing that LeMoine grabs one of the green metal stools from beneath the window and sets it beside the styling chair, so she can sit and talk more easily. They remain like that, scrolling and talking, for forty-five minutes. It's amazing how long LeMoine lingers with her clients—as if she has all the time in the world, and not two businesses to run. Eventually they decide on a medium brown with caramel highlights that will allow the gray to remain visible without dominating, and LeMoine disappears into the back room to prepare the color.

It is such an ordinary, undramatic scene. No life-changing transformation. Not even any of the pastel "fashion colors" so trendy at the moment. And yet those forty-five minutes embody a half century of change in the hair industry.

THE STORY OF HAIR has always been fascinating. Ancient Egyptian women used the juice of juniper berries to cover their gray. Ancient Roman women fermented leeches in vinegar for months, before applying the pungent paste to their hair as black dye. Marie Antoinette's gravity-defying hairdos rose as tall as four feet above her head. Native Americans believed that braided hair signified unity with the infinite.

But the story of hair has never moved as quickly as it has over the last half century. The pace of change is unprecedented in human history. And central to this story are hairstylists. Until the modern era, the intimate act of *doing* our hair—washing, cutting, styling—was a strictly private affair, attended to at home among family, or, if you were rich, with the help of servants. Not until the late 1800s did women venture out to salons and pay strangers to manage their locks. And not until the 1960s did these paid professionals become recognized as the innovators and change agents they're known as today.

Recently *The New York Times* published an essay by a woman who drove 2,130 miles across seven states, from Colorado to Manhattan, to get a haircut, she was that devoted to her hairstylist. Fifty years ago, such loyalty would have been unimaginable.

By midcentury, it was common for women to pay weekly visits to their local salon to keep their hair coiffed. Convention was king, and beauticians and hairdressers, as they were known, did their best to help everyone look like everyone else, deploying hot rollers, bobby pins, and ozone-layer-destroying amounts of hairspray. Like hospital attendants or electricians, these blue-collar tradespeople were valued for their technical skills, and not expected to have ideas of their own. Whatever extraneous talents a hairstylist might have brought to the job—an eye for proportion and scale, a knack for creating a sympathetic bond with the client—went largely unnoticed, if not by the clients themselves, then certainly by the world at large.

But in 1962, *Vogue* magazine informed its readers that when it came to hairstylists, the times had changed. Where previously the client was queen, and the hairstylist her lowly handmaiden, there to take orders and do her bidding, "Custom has swung round to a position which makes it unthinkable for a woman to say a harsh word to her hairdresser. Nor would she wish to; today's woman knows that she is only as chic as her coiffure—this is the acid test of fashion."

It was the beginning of a hair revolution. In a couple of years, Vietnam protesters would flout their long "dirty hippie" locks, and members of the Black Power movement would pick their hair into giant Afros. Starting in the 1960s, and ongoing to this day, an avalanche of social, political, and technological advances transformed the hair industry.

But before all that happened—before, perhaps, it even could happen—we had to undergo a seismic shift in how we conceive of and relate to our hair, and this shift began in the styling chair. As television and magazines furthered the reach of movie stars and celebrities, and more women tapped into the expressive capabilities of fashion, everyone began to regard their hairstylists differently. They saw that the people winding their hair onto rollers weren't mere technicians, but specialists who possessed knowledge and expertise.

"Instead of bullying the man who does her hair," *Vogue* continued, "she's apt to think of him as one of her five or six most trusted friends, sympathetic, clever with his hands, full of amusing information about one person or another, up on the avant foreign flicks, not unaware of fluctuations in the stock market, and certainly a better source of advice than the best gypsy on the block." That is, someone you might drive across seven states and 2,130 miles to go visit.

Of course, 1962 was still the early days. The hairdresser-client relationship may have been transformed—but hairstyles hadn't, not yet. *Vogue*'s feature is illustrated with photographs of women wearing enormous, elaborate hairdos involving multiple hairpieces that wouldn't look out of place at Versailles. Most notably, however, though the article is about "The World's Greatest Hairdressers," of the six assembled—all men—the most important hairdresser of the era is absent: The British wunderkind Vidal Sassoon.

IN 1954, A TWENTY-SIX-YEAR-OLD Sassoon opened his first salon, in London's posh Mayfair district, with the express intention to revolutionize hairstyling. "I wanted to eliminate the superfluous and get down to the basic angles of cut and shape," he later explained. He was interested in working *with* a woman's hair as it grew from her head, rather than torturing it into impossible, high-maintenance sculptures. His most famous innovations—the "wash-and-wear" and "five-point" cuts—were low-maintenance in the extreme. In 1968, the film director Roman Polanski paid Sassoon $5,000 to come to Hollywood and chop off Mia Farrow's long blond hair in front of reporters as a publicity stunt for *Rosemary's Baby*. Her soft, fetching, and totally effortless pixie cut immediately became a mass sensation.

Sassoon single-handedly glamorized the hair industry. For anyone who wasn't yet persuaded, he proved beyond a shadow of a doubt that being a hairstylist can involve more than just handiwork, that indeed armed with a vision, enough talent, and an ordinary pair of cutting shears, hairstylists have the potential to change not only our hair, but our lives. As he once put it, "Women were going back to work, they were assuming their own power. They didn't have time to sit under the dryer anymore." British designer Mary Quant, known for popularizing the miniskirt, was more grandiose, and rightly so: "He revolutionized the look and way of life for everyone."

This isn't to imply that inside every hairstylist is a latent genius. Rather, Sassoon's worldwide fame blew the walls off what had been a small, closed room. Formerly an option of last resort for people who couldn't afford college, the dead end of a non-career path where originality and ambition went to die, today the hair industry is a thriving, vital, and ever-growing sphere of creativity, possibility, fashion, and sophistication. This goes for everyone involved, whether a recent beauty school graduate just starting out at a local salon, or the celebrity spokesperson for a global hair-care brand.

Few people have been so well-positioned to witness, so close up, the modern hair revolution as Gwenn LeMoine. Born to two hairstylists in 1963, she was raised in a salon just as the industry began to change. As an adult, she became an industry pioneer. Today she has four decades of expertise under her belt.

2

_____

Should you want evidence that LeMoine's life is all hair, all the time, note how she describes her morning coffee: "8OR." That's the label for a hair color known as Level 8—basically, a reddish-orange hue. That is, coffee with a tiny bit of milk, just enough to take the edge off.

LeMoine lives in a two-bedroom apartment in a mostly residential neighborhood on Manhattan's Lower East Side, near the Williamsburg Bridge. "My friends call it the Jewish Old Lady Projects," she jokes. After she and her husband, a photographer from Iran, divorced in 2006, she stayed on with their two children. But since her daughter left for college in Massachusetts last year, it's just been her and her son, who attends college in Brooklyn. (Both children inherited LeMoine's interest in business: One is studying finance analytics, the other is pursuing a degree in marketing.)

Now that the children are grown, LeMoine's mornings tend to be cozy and slow. Her alarm goes off at 7:30 a.m. She hits snooze five times. The upside of being a small-business owner is that she has total control over her schedule. The downside: She works seven days a week, even if that just means checking email while on vacation (which she is good at making time for).

At 8:00 a.m. she gets up, makes coffee, feeds the animals (Jerry, a cat, and two French bulldogs, Tuesday and Russell), then returns to her bedroom, where her desk is, and starts the workday by looking at text messages. "Emergencies come in over text," she explains. "This way, if someone calls in sick, I can immediately figure out if we need a replacement."

Since 2009, when LeMoine opened Parlor's second location, across the river in downtown Brooklyn, she's essentially been running two businesses. For the next several hours she putters and works, works and putters. She looks at Parlor's social media accounts, and makes updates when necessary. These days she's creating Instagram posts about each Parlor employee that highlight various aspects of their personalities. After blending up a breakfast shake, she puts ingredients into the crockpot to eat for dinner when she gets home that night—beef korma is a favorite. Then she checks email, showers, and gets dressed.

As with any profession, working with hair begets a certain attention to dress. There's no uniform, obviously, or even a need to look a particular way. (That's the case *these* days, at least. During the "Vidal Sassoon era," as LeMoine calls it, all the male hairdressers wore dark suits with white shirts and skinny ties, as if channeling the Beatles.) In fact, one of the great pleasures of the job is that it allows for total aesthetic freedom; indeed, most people expect their hairstylists to project their own individual style. "The most important thing is to dress creatively," LeMoine says. "Have a look. It doesn't matter what it is. Just figure out what you're trying to convey with your style." The only direct advice she gives her employees on this front is to, simply, "Dress better than the client you're trying to attract."

But there are practical concerns. For one thing, it can get hot working indoors all day, in a room that's usually pretty crowded, and as LeMoine puts it, "It sucks to be sweaty and close to people." Worse, hair cuttings have a way of sticking to and smothering clothes, not to mention pricking through them like so many tiny needles. Smooth, flowy fabrics like rayon, silk, and cotton, and stiffer ones like denim, offer good protection from this occupational hazard, as does an apron, which also helps protect clothes from stains. When hair dye splashes onto fabric, it lifts out the color, leaving behind a rust-colored blotch. (LeMoine's quick fix is to color in the blotch with a black Sharpie marker. This is also one reason that she and many hairstylists tend to wear all black.)

Meanwhile, standing cutting hair all day really takes a toll on a person's back and feet. One fix is to cycle through different heel heights—making sure they're close-toed (open-toed shoes let all the hair in).

A little after 11:00 a.m., LeMoine packs her laptop and at least two pairs of shoes into a bag, and heads to work. The commute from home to the Parlor in the East Village is seven minutes if she drives, seventeen minutes if she walks; getting to the Brooklyn location is a twenty-minute drive.

Both salons open for business at noon, but LeMoine likes to arrive a little before 11:30 a.m., to conduct a "morning huddle" with the staff. Tempting as it is to envision the beauty squad shouting inspirational cheers to get psyched for the day ahead, holding scissors aloft, clipping air, in fact it's just a quiet moment for everyone to check in, ask questions, note if supplies are low.

As usual, today there are four stylists on deck, one receptionist, and one assistant (who helps everyone). At 11:30 a.m., they all stop whatever it was they'd been doing and gather as a group. LeMoine announces that she's planning to launch a new initiative to reward clients who bring in new clients. She also notes that business is usually slow in August, but that there's been an uptick in online sales of the Aveda hair and makeup products they carry. It's a brief huddle. Afterward, everyone picks up where they'd left off.

Parlor's beauty squad hails from all over the country, representing a diversity of backgrounds and upbringings. They are individuals to a one, whether liberally covered in tattoos and body piercings, or sporting a casual look that wouldn't be out of place at a suburban Starbucks. Aesthetics aside, they are united by temperament: friendly and down-to-earth, yet unfailingly professional, they have zero interest in creating a cult of personality, preferring instead to keep the focus on their clients. Also, they all came to their careers circuitously, pursuing other occupations first, before finally succumbing to what was, in most cases, their first true love, hair.

On one side of the room is Shirley Hagel, advanced creative stylist, who worked in child psychology in her native Florida before becoming a hairdresser. At the station beside her is Bryzow (she goes by one name only), senior stylist, who left her hometown of Bucks County, Pennsylvania, to earn a BA in theater design and production at the University of Evansville before moving to New York.

On the other side of the room is Alex Torres, a native New Yorker who left his Puerto Rican family to study communications in Florida, then worked in café management, before coming back to go to beauty school. Now forty, he's one of the newest members of the team, with the title of new talent stylist.

For those last few minutes before the salon opens for business, the staff is busy with final preparations. Hagel folds towels. Bryzow leans in very closely toward the mirror and trims her baby bangs. Torres sweeps the floor around his station.

Gwenn walks into the anteroom, where hair is washed and rinsed, and sits down with her laptop, taking a quiet moment before the day begins. Since taking a nasty fall last year, her knees hurt if she remains standing too long, so she sees far fewer clients than in the past.

The anteroom is a crisp, cheerful space. Three white leather and chrome pedestal chairs, each with a black-and-white strip of fabric with a Greek key pattern running down the middle, are positioned before three white sinks. The shelf along the white subway-tiled wall is piled high with neatly rolled black towels, and the floor is covered in bright turquoise penny tile. Farther on is a small room that could double as a chemistry lab. A metal table is lined with rows and rows of plastic bottles—this is where the stylists go to mix up the hair color before bringing it back out "on the floor," as the cutting and styling area is known. Helpful charts and information sheets are taped to white lacquer cabinets that rise to the ceiling. There is a list for opening and closing duties. A poster from the manufacturer about how to use Olaplex, a "bond multiplier" that helps to restore hair that's been damaged during lightening or coloring services. An Aveda flyer about upcoming educational course offerings in the Northeast. There's even a printout of a positive Yelp review that compliments one of the assistants, with "WAY TO GO ALISSA!!!" scrawled at the top.

At noon on the nose, the first client of the day walks in. By now the salon is perfectly clean and tidy, the music playing. It's as if a production crew has arranged all the sets on a stage and adjusted the lights.

Soon enough, another client arrives. Then another. Before long, as the squad combs and snips and blow-dries and consults, there's just enough buzz of convivial, energetic noise to create a pocket of privacy around each station. Every so often a word or phrase rises above the din, only to vanish back into its own private conversation: "Asbury Park," "My son's the third guy," "Art school," "Amazing, congratulations!" "When you suddenly find yourself a single parent."

Every appointment is like a short story, with a beginning, middle, and end. But the story never ends, really. Because every six weeks, or two months, or twice a year—whatever is necessary to keep a client's hair the way they want it—the story picks up where it was left off, like a never-ending series of sequels.

Nearing 3:00 p.m., LeMoine ducks out to grab a quick lunch—a bagel sandwich, perhaps, with cream cheese, avocado, jalapeño, and an egg. Eating food inside Parlor is verboten, even for her. Everyone eats their lunch elsewhere, whether just down the street in Tompkins Square Park, or in one of the many eateries that dot the neighborhood.

When she returns, she checks in with the front desk to see if there are any urgent trifles that need fixing (there aren't). Then she takes a minute to check in with Parlor's Brooklyn location. It's not easy running two operations in two separate boroughs. Fortunately, the news today is mostly good: The manager reports that one of the stylists took it upon himself to clean the basement, and she should be sure to thank him. They also discuss the work performance of a new assistant, who has great hair-cutting skills but a questionable attitude.

"I can see what she's going to bloom into, and it's not great," LeMoine tells me later. Like most effective bosses, she takes great care in making hires, most of whom she finds through word of mouth and the vast network of Aveda Institute graduates (LeMoine is an Aveda alum, and stocks only

Aveda products at the salon). In this industry, it's a rolling process—people are constantly cycling through. Naturally, she prizes great hair-cutting skills and a positive attitude, but it's also clear that she feels a genuine connection with her employees. That is yet another plus of owning your own salon—the freedom to surround yourself with people you like. A minus, of course, is having to fire someone, which inevitably happens, and which LeMoine loathes having to do. Over time, she's found that people who are naturally self-critical tend to make the best hires. They are the ones who know when they're falling behind, and what they need to do to step up. "It works better if they're critical of themselves, and it's not just up to me to point things out," she says.

After getting off the phone, she walks over to the brick wall beside the front desk and leans against it, silently surveying her domain.

Several minutes later she gestures toward me to join her. She nods her head conspiratorially, back toward the reception desk. "That's who you should be paying attention to right now," she says.

I turn to look where she's looking, and see Giovanna Berardi warmly greeting a client. From a big Italian American family on Staten Island, Berardi earned a BA in anthropology from Hunter College before pursuing hair. Now thirty-nine, she's worked at Parlor a little over a decade so far, and is one of only two employees to hold the title of advanced master stylist. She's dressed in a loose black T-shirt, cropped black pants, and white Converse low-top sneakers. A black apron simultaneously protects her clothes, and gives her otherwise casual ensemble a professional air. Her long, straight, shiny brown mane, aglow with just a few reddish highlights, could be an advertisement for the specialty she's developed over the years, what she calls "feminine, natural hair."

Berardi leads the client to her station, and the two women chat like old friends, catching up on the major headlines of the last several months—notably that the client didn't get the job she'd applied for, so is still stuck in the one she's had for what feels like way too long. When they reach Berardi's chair, the client sinks into it with obvious relief, as if it's a therapist's couch. Dressed professionally in a navy sheath dress and low heels, she appears to be in her late twenties, on her lunch hour.

"I'm just wanting a *change*, you know?" she says, shaking her head emphatically.

Berardi stands behind her and they both regard her reflection in the mirror.

Like Berardi's, the client's hair is long and thick and hangs midway down her back, with a natural wavy texture that's enhanced by the humidity. The color is natural, too, the same dark brown as her eyes, which are a few shades darker than her complexion.

Berardi nods, but remains silent, careful to not interrupt her client's train of thought. On the surface, there's not much happening here, nothing more remarkable than the type of encounter that takes place thousands if not millions of times a day, all over the world: a hairstylist and a client discussing a hairstyle. This is when I understand why LeMoine suggested that I pay attention.

The two women are engaged in the "consultation" phase of a hair appointment, when the client tells the stylist what she wants. What most of us don't realize when we're sitting in that chair is that while the conversation unfolds, the stylist is inwardly making a flurry of calculations. She is assessing the client's face shape and profile, and refamiliarizing herself with their facial features. Does the client have a strong jawline that could be enhanced, or an extra-large chin that could appear more proportional with the right style? Arresting eyes? A lovely neck? She is considering the shape of the head, the way the hair grows from it—are there cowlicks? If so, where?—as well as its texture, which is to say its density and elasticity. Even the client's height and weight are taken into consideration; for instance, big, full hair can make a heavy woman appear heavier, and overwhelm a small woman. All of these elements determine what kind of hairstyle will look best.

No two hairstylists are alike, but all good hairstylists must possess two fundamental qualities: a talent for working with their hands and emotional intelligence. The need for both is part of what sets this vocation apart from those that are purely technical. Plumbers and electricians can get away with being bona fide misanthropes, if they want. They don't require people skills to do their jobs well.

That doesn't mean all good hairstylists must excel in both realms simultaneously, however. In fact, most stylists are stronger in one capacity than they are in the other. If solving problems with your hands is one of those things that comes so naturally that you hardly need to think about it, you can coast on that innate talent for as long as you'd like, for your whole career, even. Likewise, if you're exceptionally personable and good at working with other people, at sensing their moods and hearing what they're saying even when they don't have the words to say it, that strength can compensate for a relative lack of creativity. Generally speaking, really leaning into one of those two assets is enough to attract clients and build a loyal clientele.

But those who are *very* good hairstylists, even excellent hairstylists, the ones who go on to open their own salons or become celebrities in their own right, are exceptional in both realms. They can do wonders with their hands, and they can work magic with people, creating bonds with their clients that stand the test of time. And a crucial element of this people skill, if not *the* most crucial element, is the ability to listen.

So when Berardi's client states that she wants a change, and Berardi remains silent, it's an active, not passive silence. She is paying close attention not only to the words being said, but also to *how* they are said. Hair isn't merely a biological feature—it's closely connected with our emotional selves and sense of identity. Berardi wants to take special care that she's on the same page as her client, especially if they're about to do something drastically different.

"I've decided that if I can't have a new job, at least I can have new hair," the client continues. Then she pauses, suddenly unsure of herself. "Right?"

This fleeting expression of doubt is truly the tiniest of moments, one that would go totally unnoticed if Berardi happened to turn away at that exact instant. It is easy to see how a different hairstylist might even notice but pretend that she hadn't, as if it never happened. After all, the chance to give someone "new hair" is a welcome one, part of the great fun of this job—an opportunity to be creative, challenge yourself, show what you've got, enact a transformation.

But Berardi is nothing if not attentive. "How much of a change are you thinking?" she asks cautiously. As she speaks, she gently lifts the woman's hair with her hands and lets it fall back down again. It is really quite beautiful hair.

I look back at LeMoine, who is watching the scene unfold with a satisfied smile. She has taught Berardi well. I even have the sense that her own deep knowledge of trends, personality types, and professions gives her the ability to peer into the future and predict what the outcome will be.

The client searches for the right words. "Something way brighter. Even blonde-ish maybe?—but edgy. What's that word I keep hearing? *Bayasomething?*"

Berardi laughs. Already in her mind's eye she's been scrolling through a slideshow of possible images, all of them various incarnations of *balayage*, the word that the client is searching for.

Balayage is a French word that means "to sweep" or "to paint." It's a highlighting technique that was created by French colorists in the 1970s and over the last decade has exploaded in popularity. Today it's one of the most-requested styles on the planet.

Traditional highlights start at the very base of the hair, at the root, and are meant to look seamlessly uniform and natural, as if you've always had gold strands (or butter, or caramel, or whatever other you-were-born-with-it color) glittering through your locks. The process is quite labor intensive. For decades, a perforated rubber cap was put over the head and select pieces of hair were pulled through the miniature holes (Parlor hasn't used this method for a while). These days, the stylist forgoes the cap and just separates out one thin section of hair at a time, about 1/16th of an inch wide. Either way, the hair is saturated with color, and sandwiched in a square of folded aluminum foil. A typical full head of highlights requires more than one hundred foils, which generally takes about forty-five minutes to prepare. When the prep work is finished, the color is left on the hair for up to thirty minutes, after which all of the foils are removed, and the product is rinsed out.

Balayage is different in that it doesn't require foils. It is freehand. The stylist simply paints the color onto the hair. The end result can look natural, like traditional highlights, but a different kind of natural—as if, instead of being born with this particular hue, you spent the summer on a surfboard and the sun didn't merely lightly kiss your hair, but turned big strips of it blonde. Instead of starting at the root, the color is applied an inch or more down the hair shaft, and oftentimes the very ends are left alone. No foils means the color is exposed to the air and dries more quickly, so it can go light, but never *super* light. The results run the spectrum from very subtle to quite extreme, which is when it becomes known as *ombré*, another French word, so "to shadow," a style in which the bottom portion of the hair is lighter than the top, as if someone hadn't gotten around to having her highlights touched up.

In fact, people not getting their highlights touched up is how balayage and ombré came to be mass fashions. Historically, hairstyle trends have been sparked by celebrities. Think Farrah Fawcett's feathered blonde locks in the 1970s. Or the "Rachel"—the shaggy, long, layered bob Jennifer Aniston made famous in the mid-1990s, while starring as the character Rachel Green on the TV show *Friends*; for a time, the Rachel was the most requested cut in both America and Europe.

Balayage is the result of a much larger force: the economy. In 2008, when the housing market crashed, and the world began to tumble into a global recession, many women who colored their hair simply couldn't afford to get their roots touched up. Soon enough, what had begun as an austerity measure became a bona fide trend. Very quickly, the style rose up from the streets and spread to the highest reaches of Hollywood: Alexa Chung. Jennifer Lopez. All of the Kardashians.

Of course, Berardi isn't necessarily thinking about any of this as she regards her client's hair. She's focusing on what shade of "blonde-ish" would look best with her coloring. (In a recent article, *Vogue* counted seventy shades of blonde, from "pearly white" to "chardonnay" and beyond.) She pulls her iPhone from her apron pocket and crouches beside the chair so the two women can scroll through the photos to-gether. No matter what happens, it's going to take a while. I'll check back later.

LeMoine is long gone by the time Berardi's client leaves Parlor, a woman transformed. Both salons are open until 9:00 p.m. on weekdays, but LeMoine tends to leave in the early evening, to drive to whatever location she hasn't been at all day, just to check in and say hello. On her way home she'll stop by the grocery store.

That evening, she'll rest a bit, maybe watch some TV, then go through her emails again. She's found a new, better space for the Brooklyn location, and is working with an architect to design and decorate it. She wants the exterior to be navy blue, almost black, with a pale pink door, and yesterday she went through initial swatches before giving them to the architect to choose the final shades. Tonight, while snacking on some hummus and crackers, she'll spend a bit of time shopping online for the right chairs and table. After dinner—the beef korma, for instance, that's been slow-cooking all day—she'll probably catch up on more email and TV, before heading to bed around 1:00 a.m.

3

Hair salons are such an ordinary feature of the American landscape that it's easy to think they've always existed. In fact, until the end of the nineteenth century, women did their hair at home, and only men ventured out to barbershops.

In the days before indoor plumbing was commonplace, most people washed their hair infrequently, if at all, and when they did wash it, they used the same harsh lye-based soaps meant for washing bodies. To style their hair, wealthy women relied on their servants, who would arrange elaborate updos using braids, hairpieces, and wrought-iron curling tools that were heated with fire, along with many, many hairpins. Those who couldn't afford to keep servants relied on their female relatives and friends for help. There were also independent hairdressers who made house calls, as did many traveling nurses and doctors, who provided hair skills among their medical services, and even peddled their own special hair tonics.

The original ladies' hair salon emerged in Europe with the development of court society in seventeenth-century France, when a peasant named Champagne set up shop in Paris. He was quickly shut down by the Catholic Church, on grounds of immorality. The concept didn't take hold until the mid-nineteenth century, when the rise of the department store provided a way for "respectable" women to be seen in public during the day. The most famous of these early salons was Marcel Grateau's, in Montmartre. This is where, in 1882, he eventually introduced his own invention: a new type of curling iron that produced a soft and relatively durable wave. His innovative "Marcel" waving technique replaced the popular but time-consuming fashion for curls and ringlets. "Marcelling" remained popular into the 1920s, and beauty schools continue to teach the technique to this day.

The first hair salon in America was the brainchild of a former servant named Martha Matilda Harper. Born to a poor family in Canada in 1857, she was only seven years old when her parents sent her away from home to begin her career as a live-in domestic. Among her early employers was a German doctor and herbalist who had a special interest in hair. He taught Harper the fundaments of hair health: the importance of vigorous brushing, which encourages blood flow to the hair follicles, which in turn stimulates growth, and the necessity of cleaning the scalp on a regular basis, which was a genuinely radical concept at a time when people rarely washed their hair. He also shared with her his secret herbal tonic, an organic shampoo, and instructed her to rub it vigorously into her roots, then rinse it with warm water. Under his tutelage, Harper's hair became so healthy and lustrous that eventually it grew past her waist, falling in thick chestnut waves all the way to the floor. (In photos, it flows down her back like a long, brown wedding veil.) Before the doctor died, he bequeathed Harper the secret formula.

At twenty-five, when Harper emigrated to Rochester, New York, to take a position in a minister's household, she brought along a bottle of the doctor's tonic and the secret formula. In her spare time, she worked in a shed out back, tinkering with the doctor's recipe, adding and subtracting ingredients, and testing it out on her own hair. At last she settled on a combination of sage, salt, alcohol, quinine, and cantharides (also known as Spanish fly), and came up with a chichi brand name: "Mascarao Tonique." Giving her creation a French twist was a brilliant marketing ploy at a time when France was considered the world's fashion center. Her company logo was a fat horn of plenty with its slender tip curled like a lock of hair.

In 1888, age thirty-one, armed with her proprietary hair

tonic and a life savings of $360 (the rough equivalent of $9,000 today), Harper rented a space in the fanciest commercial building downtown Rochester had to offer. To lure customers to her highly unusual "Ladies' Champooing and Hair Dressing Parlor," she posted on the front door a big photo of herself cloaked in her floor-length hair. Business was slow at first, as Harper worked to persuade the locals to consider getting their hair done in public. But it only took one visit to get them hooked.

Note that Harper did little to no hair cutting at her salon. Instead, she cleaned, dyed, and "dressed" clients' long hair with false hairpieces and padding. During the Victorian era, it was fashionable for women to grow their hair as long as they could, to the floor and beyond, if possible. Even Louisa May Alcott, author of the proto-feminist young-adult novel *Little Women*, had hair to her ankles, before a series of sicknesses she caught while nursing soldiers during the Civil War damaged her hair so badly that she had to cut it short. (Alcott later turned life into art, by having her famous character Jo chop off her "one beauty.")

While long hair was considered a central feature of feminine allure, short hair was a sign of poverty, even insanity. Often very poor women would grow out their hair in order to cut and sell it. Those who lived in the workhouses of England

and Wales were forced by their overlords to undergo a chop, as were many women who were admitted as patients to mental institutions. (Interestingly enough, though a shaved head has been considered a radical fashion statement since the punk era, it can also be a symptom of a mental breakdown, such as the one that ultimately led Britney Spears to an involuntary stay in a psychiatric ward in 2008.)

Decades of working as a servant had shown Harper the value of professional deference, or what is today known as customer service—that is, adjusting oneself to the personality of the employer, or in this case, the paying customer. She cannily founded her salon on this precept, creating a serene, restful environment in which she pampered her clients with facial and scalp massages. She even invented a special reclining chair, and had a half-circle cut out of her sinks, so that women could lean back to have their hair washed without getting shampoo in their eyes. Her range of massage, shampooing, and styling services was known as the Harper Method.

It happened that Rochester was a hub of first-wave feminist activity, and one of Harper's clients was none other than the movement's leader, Susan B. Anthony. Inspired by Anthony's philosophy that all women should be financially independent, Harper quickly expanded her business with an eye toward giving servant and factory girls a leg up. Taking a cue from the Christian Science Church, which maintained satellite operations around the country, she opened more of her own salons, single-handedly spearheading the practice of retail franchising. (Ray Kroc of McDonald's fame is often erroneously credited for this feat.) Harper dictated that the first hundred franchises could only be bought by poor women, and even loaned some of them the money to do so. At a time when women were entering the workforce in record numbers, all of her salons provided childcare, as well as evening hours, so that clients could come straight from the factory or office on their way home. Soon enough, Harper had her own beauty school, an ever-expanding line of natural hair-care products, and five hundred salons throughout North America and Europe. By the time she died in 1950, age ninety-three, she'd washed and styled the hair of tens of thousands of people, ranging from regular working women to first ladies, including Grace Coolidge, Jacqueline Kennedy, and Lady Bird Johnson, and even one sitting president, Woodrow Wilson.

HARPER MAY HAVE INVENTED the American hair salon, but she wasn't the only beauty tycoon of her era. The other was Madam C.J. Walker, known as the first female self-made millionaire in America, and one of the most successful African American business owners to this day.

She was born Sarah Breedlove, in 1867, on a cotton plantation near Delta, Louisiana, the fifth child to enslaved people who had only recently been freed, and the first in her family to be free-born. In 1887, after her husband died, she moved with her toddler daughter, A'Lelia, to St. Louis, Missouri, where her brothers worked as barbers. Once there, she found a job as a washerwoman, which paid enough for her to send A'Lelia to school. She also met the man who would become her second husband, Charles J. Walker, who worked in advertising.

In the 1890s, Walker developed a scalp disorder that caused her to lose most of her hair. In the hopes of improving her condition, she began experimenting with store-bought and homemade remedies, and eventually developed her own. She decided to start her own business. Her husband persuaded her to go by the name Madam C.J. Walker—a more recognizable brand name than Sarah Breedlove—and created advertisements for her treatments. In 1907, they traveled together throughout the South promoting her exclusive line of African American hair-care products.

Walker was an immediate sensation. In 1908, she opened her own factory and a beauty school, both in Pittsburgh, Pennsylvania. Business boomed so rapidly that in 1910, the

Madam C.J. Walker Manufacturing Company moved its base of operations to Indianapolis, Indiana, and expanded to include cosmetics and a training program for sales beauticians, aka "Walker Agents." In 1913, the couple divorced, and by 1916 Walker and A'Lelia were established in a townhouse in Harlem, where they became central actors in the cultural and political changes taking place there. With her company now worth millions, she donated money to causes devoted to improving the lives of African Americans, from educational scholarships to homes for the elderly, as well as the National Association for the Advancement of Colored People, and the National Conference on Lynching.

In 1919, Walker died an early death, at age fifty-one, of hypertension. Her business was valued at more than $1 million. She'd just put the final touches on Villa Lewaro, the lavish, thirty-four-room mansion she'd had built in Irvington-on-Hudson, New York. Today the estate is a National Historic Landmark, and its current owners hope to turn it into a house museum.

As PIONEERS OF THE hair-care industry, both Harper and Walker set into motion a series of changes that picked up speed as the century progressed, evolving so rapidly, in comparison to previous decades, that it may have been difficult for other entrepreneurs even as bold and progressive as they were to keep up.

The first big change had occurred in the 1910s, when the "bob" haircut started popping up on the heads of movie stars. By the 1920s, the new fashion was sweeping the nation. Women in small towns and big cities alike shocked their parents and society at large by chopping their long hair to their chins. The new look was blunt, geometric. On the one hand, the short, boyish cut liberated women from the trappings of conventional femininity that had heretofore been signaled by long, flowing tresses. On the other hand, it chained them to a new grooming ritual: more frequent visits to the hair salon for regular trims.

In 1920, there were roughly five thousand hair salons in America. Over the next four years, sixteen thousand more opened their doors. In 1924 alone, over the course of a single week, thirty-five hundred women had their hair bobbed (smelling salts were on hand because so many women fainted). At Coe College in Cedar Rapids, Iowa, a campus visit from the famous poet Edna St. Vincent Millay—who'd recently bobbed her long flame-red locks—shot the percentage of students with bobbed hair from nine percent to sixty-three percent.

It was a stressful and confusing time for professional hairdressers, who'd been trained to arrange and curl long hair, not to cut it. Because so many were slow to come around to the fact that short hair for women was here to stay, a large number of barber shops turned into salons, to meet the demand. Now that barbers were, by necessity, also ladies' hairdressers, the formerly all-female profession received a boost in status.

And so the modern salon—that is, the salon as we know it—took off. A 1931 hairdressing guide listed the six key areas of a salon: the premises; the facade; the front shop (now known as reception); hairdressing saloons; workroom/laboratory/storeroom; offices and toilets.

In these temples to beauty, hairstyles became more various and elaborate. Whether bobbed or kept long, throughout the 1930s manufactured curls and waves were de rigueur, thanks largely to the rise of Hollywood. Jean Harlow's platinum coif set the standard—no matter that the requisite layered haircuts, weekly application of bleach and peroxide, and painstaking formation of pin curls (small coils wound by hand, secured with bobby pins, and left to set overnight) were quite time-consuming.

When World War II broke out in 1939, and women took over the factory jobs once held by men, styles changed yet again. Waves became softer, and "rolls" ubiquitous: rather than sleeping with a head full of pin curls, a woman would wind a few big sections of hair into large cylindrical rolls that she'd pin and spray and wear out just like that—no need to set them—frequently with a net-like "snood" protecting the curls in back. For a "Victory Roll," she'd wind all the hair in back into one tight sausage, often using the top of an old stocking as a headband. Rolls were relatively easy to do, and protected long hair from falling into machinery. After working all day, a woman could take off her snood or headband, brush out the curls, and step out to a dance hall looking fantastic.

During the 1950s, hair got bigger, higher, and fussier. Hairdressers and clients alike were addicted to their weekly appointments—as well as permanents, hairspray, and back combing. By the 1960s, the beehive reigned supreme. Ironically, though this style took a lot of time to achieve, once it was done it could stay put for weeks. Rumor has it that in 1962 a high school student in Canton, Ohio, left her beehive to its own devices for so long that a family of cockroaches moved in. (She didn't realize it until a classmate spotted a trickle of blood on the back of her neck.)

Then came Vidal Sassoon. He opened his first salon in America in 1965, and was immediately summoned by the New York State Cosmetology Board to take the state licensing exam. Sassoon was outraged, and refused, calling the exam "asinine and obsolete." He thought it ridiculous that the test required methods such as finger waving and reverse pin curling—styles that women hadn't worn since the golden era of silent film. "I simply cannot take it on the grounds that it violates everything I've worked for for twenty-one years," he told *The New York Times*.

Sassoon closed his Manhattan salon and returned to London, but the domino effect of change that he'd started was already taking place. It was just a few short strides from his effortless "wash-and-wear" cuts to the "natural" ethos of the late 1960s and early 1970s, when men and women alike, black and white, grew their hair long, and styled it into big Afros or let it hang loose around their shoulders. And so hairstyles cycled—from the giant, decadent perms of the 1980s to the straight shiny blowouts of the 1990s—and continued on into the twenty-first century—back and forth, back and forth—until now, when for the first time in recorded history literally anything goes: long, short, big, flat, shiny, nappy, coiled, sleek, pink, purple, weaves, extensions, braids, with no end in sight.

eMoine grew up in a family of hairdressers. Both of her parents cut hair; indeed, they met each other while in beauty school, when they were twenty years old. Her father's mother attended beauty school *with* him—it had always been on her bucket list, and when she was diagnosed with leukemia she decided now was the moment, and it would be a nice way to spend time with her son. When she died at forty-three, her husband—LeMoine's grandfather—remarried a hairdresser. LeMoine's father even owned his own beauty parlor for nearly five decades.

Her father's business, John Fredericks for Beauty, in West St. Paul, Minnesota, was a simple local service salon. "An old lady salon," LeMoine says. The only employees were Gwenn's parents and a woman they hired to manage the reception desk. The place was stylish, though, at least in the late 1960s, when it opened for business. Shag carpeting covered the floors, and the walls were made over in green driftwood-effect fake paneling. Seven styling chairs upholstered in royal blue pleather faced a row of big gold mirrors with Moroccan detailing. On the other side of the room, ten chairs with hood hair dryers affixed to the tops were arranged in a giant U.

Back then, most women kept a standing appointment at their local salon, usually once a week. Let's say your day was Tuesday. Your stylist would wash your hair, wind it onto rollers, then lead you to the hair-drying area, where you'd sit under the hood for twenty or so minutes, heat blasting your head. Once your hair was dry, the stylist would take out the rollers and brush and spray your hair into a style intended to last until your next appointment. (That is, provided you didn't ruin it by getting it wet, whether by getting caught in an unexpected rain shower or by exercising too strenuously, in which case you'd have to book an emergency appointment to get it fixed.) For women who didn't leave the house to work, but instead stayed home to raise their children, this weekly appointment was a welcome treat, a chance to flip through magazines and gossip with friends.

Being at the salon was a treat for young LeMoine, as well. She loved it so much that she eagerly anticipated school vacations just so she could spend every day there. For Christmas, they'd put up a fake tree, flocked with white, and decorate it with combs and clips as ornaments. Each morning, she'd accompany her parents to the parlor with a plate of cookies she and her mother had baked the night before. As the day progressed, she'd help out in whatever way was needed—emptying ashtrays, helping to take rollers out, answering the phone. Because the giant hood hair dryers of the time were monstrously loud, and the women therefore couldn't chat with one another as their rollers set, Gwenn would pass a plate of cookies as they sat waiting, immobilized. Her father had a very talkative, relationship-based method of interacting with his clients, and because of this they knew everything about her there was to know. She basked in their attention. It felt wonderful to spend all day in a warm, convivial place full of women fussing over her.

And yet, when LeMoine grew up, her father actively discouraged her from joining the family business. The money just wasn't good enough, he explained. Her mother wasn't any more encouraging; as soon as she could, she quit cutting hair to stay home with her four young children. So even though the hair salon was LeMoine's favorite place in the world to be, she never dreamed she'd become a hairdresser herself.

Besides, her parents hoped their oldest child would be the first in the family to graduate from college. LeMoine certainly had the chops. She was bright and creative, entrepreneurial even, crafting little dolls and stuffed animals and selling them to people. Once, when she was eight or nine, she got hold of a bunch of dog food samples and sold them to the neighbors, in spite of the fact that each bag was clearly marked with the word *FREE*. (LeMoine's mother made her give everyone their money back, and let them keep their samples.) It seemed a no-brainer that this little go-getter would grow up to make them all proud.

That is, until LeMoine hit adolescence, and her creative outlets became a little more . . . creative.

"When she was sixteen she ran away with the circus!" says Sarah Jones, LeMoine's youngest sister, also a hairdresser, who's worked at Parlor for the last twelve years.

We're sitting on a bench in the front window of Parlor's Brooklyn location, waiting for LeMoine to finish a meeting with her bookkeeper. She's sitting just a few feet away from us, and not surprisingly, she's been keeping an ear open.

"It was the state fair, not the circus!" LeMoine interjects, looking up from her laptop and laughing. "Sarah always tells everyone the circus!"

Unlike her East Village salon, which LeMoine designed from the ground up, this one came readymade. Everything is blonde wood, from the walls to the floors to the impossibly high ceiling, projecting a chic Scandinavian feel. Though larger in terms of square feet than the East Village address, here there are only four stations instead of seven. Each is a boxy white leather and chrome pedestal chair cased in blonde wood, set facing a wall of mirrors and built-in cabinets. At the back of the room, three similar chairs are arranged in front of three white sinks. In the middle of the room is the front desk.

The story goes as such: By 1979, LeMoine's independent streak had flourished into a full-on rebellion. By now she thought of herself as an artist and was completely bored with high school. She started cutting classes and doing drugs. Not surprisingly, she also began doing wild things with her hair. First she cut her hair short and shaved lines into her head. When that grew out, she gave herself an undercut and arranged the remaining hair on top into a mohawk.

"My parents were so controlling, so restrictive! If you tell me what to do, I want to know *why*. Tell me why. Of course, I also just wanted out of Minnesota so bad," she laughs, turning back to her bookkeeper.

Jones finishes the story. The annual Minnesota State Fair has been one of the most popular tourist destinations in the region going back to the nineteenth century. In recent years, upwards of two million people have shown up for twelve days of live music, amusement park rides, and livestock competitions, to name just a few of the many attractions.

That fall, it was a great lineup: Styx, Willie Nelson, KC and the Sunshine Band. LeMoine went with some of her friends, and decided to trip on LSD for the first time. Unbeknownst to her, she was given an enormous dose, enough for two people. She got so high that she told her best friend she was going to run away. Also unbeknownst to her, her friend, rightfully worried, found a payphone and called LeMoine's parents to alert them to their daughter's plan. Within an hour they showed up at the fair with two state troopers and began to search for their daughter. When news of this unexpected turn of events reached LeMoine, she decided to turn herself in to the police. Needless to say, she was very high.

What had begun as a heedless adolescent lark became a major turning point in LeMoine's life. After that, her parents came down even harder than they had before, and sent LeMoine away to a chemical dependency treatment center. She was there for six months. While there, she learned how to identify her feelings, and what she could and could not change about herself. When she returned home, she wasn't any more interested in her schoolwork than she had been before, but she was better at managing herself and her relationship with her parents.

In 1981, LeMoine learned that she couldn't graduate high school on schedule, with the rest of her class. She'd failed French. As her friends went off to college, she stayed home and got a job at Accessible Space Incorporated, a national nonprofit organization that provides housing and services for people with physical disabilities, seniors, and veterans. LeMoine loved her job as a personal attendant and her wild hairstyles were a hit with her many clients.

Meanwhile, she tried to figure out what to do with the rest of her life. First she thought about going to art school, but her father persuaded her that she'd never make enough money as an artist, and deep down she knew that she wouldn't be happy if she wasn't able to make money.

For a while she thought about becoming an architect— she'd always been good at geometry, and thought that would translate well to structures and buildings. Her father said

OK, let's go over to the University of Minnesota and get a course catalog and see what kind of classes you'd have to take. When she saw how much math the degree required, she balked.

Finally, the following year, she had the "Ah-hah!" moment that changed her life forever.

She'd taken a new job, at an insurance agency, processing computer data for steam boilers. She became good friends with one of her coworkers, and began spending a lot of time with him and his boyfriend, a hairdresser, and their circle of friends, mostly gay men who also aspired to become artists. Compared to her frugal, practical parents, these new friends seemed captivatingly sophisticated, knowledgeable about fashion and luxury, and they welcomed LeMoine into their world, teaching her everything they knew.

She was particularly drawn to her friend's boyfriend, the hairdresser. He was so stylish; fabulous, really. LeMoine began bringing him drawings of haircuts she wanted. One night, while they were all out at a bar in downtown Minneapolis, her turned to her and said, "Have you ever thought of becoming a hairdresser yourself?"

For a flash moment LeMoine was confused. Her father was a hairdresser, and she didn't want to be anything like him. Then she realized what her friend was saying.

"You mean—be a hairdresser like *you*?" she asked, incredulous. It had never occurred to her that she could be nearly as fabulous as the person standing before her.

LeMoine felt as if she'd just been tossed a life preserver. All this time she'd been floating at sea, and now, all of a sudden, she knew she was going to be OK, that her life had a direction after all.

Her parents didn't exactly agree. When she announced the next day that she intended to go to beauty school, they told her they wouldn't pay for it, that she was "a bad investment."

Whether or not their resistance fueled her fire, or she was ablaze enough already, is impossible to say. Once the idea caught hold, nothing was going to stand in her way. And that wasn't all. Then and there, LeMoine decided that she wasn't going to be just a regular old hairdresser, like her parents. She was going to be someone who was really, really good at it.

Right around this time, Prince was filming his movie *Purple Rain*, and LeMoine got a part as an extra. When her boss at the insurance company wouldn't give her the time off, she quit. No, she didn't get to meet Prince during the filming, but it was definitely an auspicious start to the rest of her life.

5

LeMoine didn't know it at the time, but 1982, the year she enrolled in beauty school, happened to coincide with the next major turning point in the hair industry.

Whether Vidal Sassoon's effortless hairstyles in the 1960s predicted or helped to create a widespread interest in all things natural, by the 1970s the hippie counterculture had taken hold. The popular anti-establishment styles actually required some effort—many white women used a standard clothing iron to achieve their "natural" stick-straight tresses, while black women (and men) meticulously styled and moisturized their curls into Afros, sleeping in do-rags or satin night caps to protect them at night. But the appetite for natural ingredients—in food and beauty treatments alike—was unadulterated. All over the country, to escape the scourge of pesticide-laden produce and chemical products peddled by supermarkets, people organized to open their own co-op and/or "health-food" stores, where they could count on finding organic groceries—whether to eat, or turn into a homemade face scrub.

In 1970, an Austrian hairstylist named Horst Rechelbacher, who owned a small chain of salons called Horst & Friends in Minneapolis, Minnesota, attended a lecture by an Indian guru about Ayurvedic medicine, which uses herbs and plants to create wellness. He was so inspired by the talk that he wound up traveling to India, where he spent six months learning everything he could about the herbs, oils, and plants used in Ayurvedic health care and aromatherapy. When he returned, like Martha Matilda Harper and Madam C.J. Walker before him, he used his home as a laboratory to tinker and create his own recipes. His first successful formula was for a clove shampoo that he made in his kitchen sink. Soon enough, he'd also created cherry-bark hair conditioners, and lip glosses made from acai berry and purple corn.

In 1978, Rechelbacher founded the world's first all-natural beauty company, called Aveda. (The name was derived from the Sanskrit word *Ayurveda*, which means "science of life.") His signature pitch was, "Don't put anything on your skin that you wouldn't put in your mouth"—which he often demonstrated by drinking his hair spray. Over the next two decades, Aveda became so successful that it spawned countless imitators and in 1997 was bought by the multinational beauty company Estée Lauder for a reported $300 million.

Central to Aveda's success was its educational arm. As the company grew alongside Rechelbacher's chain of salons, he couldn't find enough hairstylists he deemed qualified enough to work for him. So in 1982, he founded the Horst Education Center in downtown Minneapolis. He certainly wasn't the first beauty tycoon to open his own beauty school, but as a pioneer of the natural hair-care movement who prized creativity above all else, he brought a decidedly different approach to teaching hair care.

THERE ARE NEARLY AS many ways to *be* a professional hairstylist as there are hairstyles, but in America there is a single path to getting there: graduate from a state-approved beauty or cosmetology school, then pass the state licensing exam (in English).

The word *state* is crucial here: When it comes to beauty school, the state rules.

In America, a driver's license is issued by the state, not the federal government. The same goes for a cosmetology license. Every state has its own cosmetology licensing board that decides how many hours you need to stay in school to train to become a licensed professional, and what questions you'll be asked on your licensing exam.

The requisite amount of school time ranges from one thousand hours (such as in New York and Georgia) to twenty-three hundred hours (Oregon), with most states requiring sixteen hundred hours. For a full-time student, that means anywhere from nine months to fifteen months of school.

Several states, including Alaska, Maine, and Utah, recognize "apprenticeship hours"—that is, working as an assistant to a licensed professional—in place of beauty school. Also, in some states there are high schools that allow juniors and seniors to take courses in cosmetology that count toward their overall training hours once they enroll in beauty school.

It is complicated, to say the least. But before we go on, a note about terminology, which complicates things even further.

A "barber" is someone who cuts, trims, and styles head and facial hair for primarily male clients. That's it.

A "hairstylist" or "hairdresser" is trained to offer those same services, as well as those used primarily by female clients, including coloring, relaxing, and curling.

A "cosmetologist" is trained to do all of the above—along with a variety of spa and beauty services that include makeup, nails, and some skin care. LeMoine is a cosmetologist. But, like most cosmetologists, she refers to herself as a "hairstylist."

As if that weren't confusing enough, there are two types of schools where one can be trained in the art of doing hair: a cosmetology school or a beauty school. In conversation, however, most people conflate the two terms, and refer to "cosmetology school" as "beauty school."

Officially, a cosmetology school teaches a comprehensive curriculum that encompasses hair design, makeup artistry, nail technology, and skin care, while a beauty school teaches only a single one of those programs. Basically, a cosmetology school is always a beauty school, but a beauty school is not always a cosmetology school.

In America, all professional hairstylists must attend some kind of hair school and pass the state licensing exam. Whether that hair school is a cosmetology school that offers the comprehensive cosmetology shebang (hair, skin, nails), or a beauty school that focuses only on hair, varies by state. (A few states have stand-alone "hair design" license options—that is, a "traditional" hairstyling license that is separate from a cosmetology license—but they're pretty rare.)

A school's tuition is also determined by its location. A recent survey by Beauty Schools Marketing Group found that the cost of cosmetology school in a large city averages between $10,000 and $20,000, while the same comprehensive cosmetology program in a rural area could cost closer to $6,500. Add to that the cost of textbooks.

Many of these schools participate in federal financial aid programs, but if you're considering applying for assistance, be mindful that it can take many months for the paperwork to go through before you even learn if you'll be awarded a financial aid package, so substantial planning ahead is required. Requirements for grants and scholarships include already being accepted or enrolled in a cosmetology program, and legal residency in the United States (either by citizenship status or student visa for resident immigrants). There are also scholarships and grants available through several national organizations and cosmetology companies.

GETTING INTO BEAUTY SCHOOL is blessedly uncomplicated. The only requirements are that you be at least sixteen years old and have a high school diploma (or its equivalent). If only the rest were so easy!

Most people think that beauty school will be a breeze. Nothing could be further from the truth. Nearly every hairstylist I interviewed admitted that beauty school wound up being a lot more difficult than they'd thought it would be. You must attend classes in subjects ranging from human anatomy to sanitation, and learn about the chemicals used for various processes, from coloring hair to making straight hair curly or curly hair straight. You are also required to log many hours of hands-on practice. This goes for wherever you happen to be enrolled. Indeed, dropout rates for beauty schools tend to be high. Unlike enrolling in a state university that's known far and wide as a "party school," the sort of place where, should you choose, you can skate through without worrying too much about your grades, there's no such thing as an "easy" beauty school.

That said, some beauty schools do have better reputations than others, for teaching their students more thoroughly, and with more sophistication. There are four hundred and seventy-five beauty schools in New York state alone—but of those, only a handful are widely considered to be excellent. Among them is the Aveda Institute, which is often referred to as "the Harvard of beauty school."

WHEN LEMOINE ENROLLED AT the first Aveda school in 1982, she was among the first class of incoming students. "It was so inspiring and high-fashion and *cool*," LeMoine remembers about the early days of Aveda. "It was such a revolutionary time for the company, when everything was just beginning. Going to beauty school there was as good as going to art school, but it was a craft that could be utilized."

For her first year, she attended classes from 8:00 a.m. until 5:00 p.m., then worked as a cook at an after-hours club in downtown Minneapolis called Ya Gadz! from 8:00 p.m. to 5:00 a.m. It was an astonishingly brutal schedule. "You know, twenty-one-year-old me thought I could do anything," LeMoine laughs. Fifteen hundred and fifty hours of school later—or, approximately eleven months—she was done.

In 1987, the school moved to its current eighty-eight-thousand-square-foot flagship location in northeast Minneapolis, and was renamed the Aveda Institute. Today there are more than sixty schools in the Aveda network across North America, nearly all of which are owned by independent parties that use Aveda's education curriculum. More than seven thousand students graduate from the network each year. Aveda is rightly proud of its job-placement rate. Seventy-four percent of all Aveda graduates go on to get jobs in the industry, which is fourteen percent above the creditor requirement.

SAM OSLYN, ONE OF LeMoine's newest hires at Parlor's Brooklyn location, graduated from the Aveda Institute in Manhattan last year.

Clean-cut and energetic, Oslyn looks younger than his twenty-three years, while his precise-yet-gentle manner make him seem older. When I meet him at the salon, he is dressed stylishly in a slim black T-shirt, slim black pants slightly tapered and cropped at the ankle, and black-and-white-checkered Vans. He often changes the color of his hair, but right now it's his born-with-it brown, kept short.

Sam grew up on Martha's Vineyard, in Oak Bluffs, the child of schoolteachers. He loved school himself, and after high school enrolled in Georgetown University in Washington, DC, to study international relations and Spanish. His plan was to join the Foreign Service.

He only stayed two years, though. He didn't like DC, how buttoned-up it was—"More like Martha's Vineyard than Martha's Vineyard," he says, rolling his eyes.

During his sophomore year he landed an internship at an advertising agency in New York City and basically never left. It was one of those situations where learning what he didn't like—sitting at a desk from nine to five, communicating with coworkers primarily via email—allowed him to accept what he does like, which is to work closely with people and have meaningful interactions. "I love talking to people, learning about them," he says. "I love physical touch, and I love that other touch, figuring out what makes people tick, or letting them just have a moment." Also: hair.

He'd always loved doing hair. It was a passion, a hobby. For his little sister's prom, he did her hair and that of all of her friends. In college he was famous for his $5 fades.

Even so, he was the last to know that he'd go to beauty school. It was his best friend from home, who was in school in New York City, who said, "You always joke about hair school, but I think you'd actually really like it."

On a whim, Oslyn Googled "best hair school in NYC." The results: Aroja, Aveda, Oribe. After conducting a bit of internet research, he chose Aveda for how it mirrors his own values. "It was organic and free trade before organic and free trade were trendy," he says. "They don't use harsh chemicals. They give back to the community. The salon experience is holistic, involving chakras and comforting teas. All this stuff is part of the mission statement, and it trickles down to the community."

That was November 2015. In December, Oslyn visited the Aveda Institute in Manhattan, took a tour, and talked with an admissions adviser about options. The school operates on a rolling cycle of admissions every couple of months, with four groups of students in school at once, progressing consecutively through the four stages of study. Students can choose to enroll full-time, part-time, or just nights. There's no official admissions interview, just an entrance interview that checks for baseline reading and math skills.

Because he could afford to, and because at this point he couldn't wait to get going, Oslyn signed up to be a full-time student starting the very next cycle, which began after the holidays, in February 2016. For seven straight months he'd be there Tuesday through Saturday, 9:00 a.m. to 5:00 p.m., forty hours a week. That's how long it would take to accrue the one thousand hours of training required by the New York State Licensing Board.

The state is extraordinarily strict about keeping track of each student's hours. At Aveda, people signed in using a hand-print system every morning. "There was usually a big rush for everyone to get their hand scanned before 9:00 a.m.," Oslyn says. "Then we'd filter into the classroom. It was really kind of a fun moment. All adults, all walks of life, drinking our coffee, getting our minds together for the day." He especially appreciated how Aveda's instructors open each day with a wellness ritual, whether an aroma experience with wintergreen body oil, say, or just taking a moment to do deep breathing exercises.

The program is a combination of textbook and hands-on learning. The first two stages are in the classroom, where you're taught "all the boring dry stuff you have to get through," he says, laughing. "The general consensus is that the beginning can be a little bit of a drag. You're so excited to get at all the fun stuff you paid for—your kit, your mannequin. But instead, you're looking at slide shows of blood contamination information. What to do if you cut your finger, or drop your comb on the floor. Stuff you'd never thought of before."

A "kit" is an assortment of all the basic cosmetology supplies necessary to cutting hair. All students must have one, no matter the state or the school. Some schools supply this kit with the price of tuition; others require that the students assemble their own. A complete kit generally costs between $1,500 and $2,500, depending on the school, the state, and where the supplies were purchased (if they weren't preprovided by the school).

The standard hair kit typically includes combs, brushes, shears, scissors, razors, items for mixing and applying hair color, clips of all kinds, sprays, a blow-dryer and diffusers, flat iron, curling irons, perm supplies, hair dyes, apron, capes, coloring caps, mirrors, and at least one mannequin head to practice on. Students can choose whether their kit comes in a rolling suitcase, a rolling aluminum case, or a rolling plastic kiosk with drawers.

The workload is intense. Oslyn's class started out with twenty-two students, but by the second phase there were only eleven left (all of whom graduated).

"It's tough," he says. "There's a lot of book work and testing up front. A lot of people are in their forties, going back to school as a second career, and they haven't taken a test in twenty years. They're working and going to school and doing a million things, and especially because of the rigidity of the attendance requirement, you have to be one hundred percent on it."

The primary textbook at most beauty schools is *Milady Standard Cosmetology.* It's been in publication since 1938, and has since been updated and revised many times. The editors aren't exaggerating when they say in the preface that "many of the world's most famous, sought-after, successful, and artistic professional cosmetologists have studied this very book!"

Milady is a 1,082-page doorstopper packed with photos, illustrations, and diagrams that cover basically everything there is to know about cosmetology. There are step-by-step instructions for how to shampoo and condition a person's hair and how to massage the scalp. There are helpful tips for things you've likely never thought about before, such as a warning to never lend out your shears. (Everyone cuts hair using a certain amount of hand pressure, and lending can lead to reconditioning the blades, which may make them not cut correctly for you.)

Though dense with information, the book is written in clear, helpful language and includes lots of creative ways to explain things. For instance, a section about "graduated haircuts" includes an illustration of a hand holding an open telephone book by the spine, with the pages flopping down on either side. "The edges of the pages make a beveled line, just like a graduated haircut," the text reads.

Chapter titles range from "Life Skills" to "General Anatomy and Physiology" to "The Salon Business," and everything in between, including "Basics of Chemistry" and "Basics of Electricity." All sorts of trade secrets are divulged, such as the fact that light and warm hair colors create the illusion of volume, dark and cool colors do the opposite, and dimension, or depth, is achieved when the hair is a mix of both. Or that yak hair blends beautifully with human hair and is often used in hair extensions. Or that a general guide for classic proportion is that the hair shouldn't be wider than the center of the shoulders.

Students learn that hair type is categorized by two defining characteristics: wave patterns and hair texture. All humans have one of four wave patterns: straight, wavy, curly, and extremely curly. The basic hair textures are fine, medium, and coarse, with a hair-per-square-inch density that ranges from very thin to very thick. These qualities determine how hair behaves when it's styled. For instance, wavy, fine hair can be easily straightened, but loses volume in the process, whereas diffusing it will give it a fuller appearance. Extremely curly, medium hair tends to look wider rather than longer as it grows.

There are tutorials for how to recognize the seven basic face shapes, and tips on how to work with various features. For instance, wide-set eyes, which are usually found on round or square faces, look more proportional with a higher half bang, which creates length in the face. Likewise, a crooked nose looks less prominent with an asymmetrical, off-center hairstyle than a symmetrical one.

For the first two weeks of beauty school, after spending the morning working with the book, Oslyn and his class would break for an hour, always clocking in and out. "The lunchroom was a fun place," Oslyn says. "The myth of beauty school is that you're sitting around doing everyone's hair all the time, but actually you're not allowed to have your hair done by another student while you're in training. You're required to record what skills you're working on hour by hour, and if you're having your hair done that means you're not technically working on any of your skills during that time so it wouldn't count toward your training hours! Instead, people just hung out and talked. Those who were working jobs while going to school would be napping in the corner. Others would be FaceTiming with their kids, or just doing their beauty school homework." (Note that when LeMoine went to beauty school in Minnesota, there were no such provisions against doing a student's hair. This is probably because the program is nearly twice the length of the one in New York.)

By week two, "We busted out our mannequins and went through step-by-step instructions with haircutting and styling. That was great," he says. As the weeks progressed, they did more and more mannequin work, and dealt less with books, until finally, in the third phase, they started "cutting hair for real on the floor. This is the awesome fun part where all the magic happens," he says. "You're cutting your teeth, finally getting to do everything you've been wanting to do."

Like many beauty schools, Aveda offers a steep discount to clients who book appointments with students. These clients, who are referred to among students and faculty as "models," are made to sign a waiver. "It's a great way to get professional color services, and not use box dye at home, but it does come with a level of uncertainty," he admits. By the final phase, he was working with models five days a week.

There was usually time for three to five models a day. At each step, an educator would come over to supervise. Haircut—check. Blow-dry—check. All told, an appointment would take about ninety minutes, fully double the length of a standard appointment in a salon.

"It's so much fun, but it's also part of the training for the human experience of it all. How to deal with a client. How to have those interpersonal skills. They tell you what not to talk about—religion and politics, basically. I didn't understand the importance of that at the time, but more recently, as I've been developing relationships with clients, I've definitely had situations where I put my foot in my mouth and regretted it. So I've gone back to that rule. No religion, no politics."

OSLYN FINISHED SCHOOL IN September 2016. "It was sort of a letdown, actually!" he says. "Very abrupt. There's no graduation day or anything. Because people are enrolled on a rolling basis, you don't even know who is finishing when. You literally just hit your one thousandth hour, down to the second, and they're like, 'Cool, you're done, good luck, 'bye.'"

Oslyn's next step was to take the licensing exam. The exam

is in two parts—a written test and a practical portion—and you must do them on different days. Because it can take a long time to get your test dates, graduates are given a temporary certificate of completion that lasts only six months—just enough to show a potential employer that you're legit, and to leave you enough time to confirm your dates. Even though Oslyn went online to make his appointment the very day school ended, the soonest one he could get was seven months later, in April 2017. "You never know when they'll happen, so I recommend staying on top of that," he says.

In New York, the exams are held in convention centers and schools around the city, always in a different place. His would be at the New York State Licensing Center, in Chinatown. It cost $15 to sign up.

The day of Oslyn's written exam was one of the first warm days of spring, but incredibly windy. He'd made sure to study, using the flash cards he'd relied on during school, and felt very well prepared. Technically, there can be a question about any word used in the *Milady* textbook, on any topic. Even though Oslyn's focus was on hair, he also had to be ready to answer questions about nail health, makeup, and skincare.

The exam began at 10:00 a.m. on a Tuesday. He arrived early. "It was a little intimidating, and everything was gray and dull," he said. "There were probably one hundred and fifty people in a big room waiting to take the test. Everyone was nervous. I cracked jokes with a couple of people to break the tension."

A few minutes before the exam started a proctor corralled everyone by last name into a giant test room. "It was the biggest test classroom you could have," he recalls. Because a lot of people there don't speak English as their first language, the proctors take time helping the students fill out all the necessary identification information.

"The girl sitting behind me was there taking the exam for the third time," Oslyn remembers. "That made me really sad. I could tell she was passionate and really wanted to do it, but something wasn't clicking for her. She probably just wasn't good at succeeding in a dry testing environment."

The exam is one hundred "rapid-fire, no-frills" questions, multiple choice. Like any standardized test, you fill in the bubbles with a #2 pencil. You have an hour to take it. It took Oslyn about twenty minutes. When he finished, he made sure to double-check that he'd filled in all the bubbles.

The exam is pass/fail; you need to answer at least seventy out of one hundred questions correctly. Oslyn received his results in less than a week. He'd passed.

———

ANY COSMETOLOGY PROGRAM IS directly teaching students to take the practical exam, so this portion of the accrediting process is much easier. Oslyn had practiced it ten times already in school. Over the months since, he'd looked it up online. "You can literally Google the website and practice at home," he said. "You know exactly what they're going to ask you to do."

Because the practical exam lasts roughly four hours, and is made up of many movable parts, they're held less frequently. Luckily, Oslyn was able to take his one week after his written exam. It was held at 3:00 p.m. on a Thursday in a technical high school in the Bronx.

He showed up with a giant duffle bag—his full kit, with everything he needed, including plenty of Barbicide disinfectant and Band-Aids. Proving that you're following health and safety protocols to a T is a big part of this exam. He also had his trusty mannequin head, Samantha #2, a famous version that's issued in beauty school as part of your kit. The one you use for the test has to be unused, so he'd bought himself a new one for $40. (You can bring any human hair mannequin you'd like, so long that it has long hair that's never been cut, colored, or textured.)

This time it was a much smaller group, because the proctors need to directly watch the test takers. There were twenty test takers in all, overseen by four proctors, who are licensed cosmetologists.

Each student was given a station with a mirror set-up. "The test began with a forty-minute haircut. The proctor tells you what kind. It was a round layered cut, pretty standard."

As they cut, the proctors circled, making sure everyone was using the proper body positioning and tools. They check for demonstrations of twelve different skills.

"It was a lot less dry and intimidating than the setting of the written exam," Oslyn remembers. "The proctors kept it professional, but they were also being reassuring. You got the sense that they wanted you to succeed, which was really nice."

Once the haircut was finished, they moved through a series of different technical tests, from applying perm rods to setting a pin curl on a small section to properly doing a round brush blow-dry. "The second portion was style based," he says. "I found that fun. Kind of interesting."

He was less enthusiastic about the chemical services portion of the exam. "It's so messy and gross," he says. "You don't use real color or relaxers for the exam. It's not about actually styling the hair, just showing that you know the proper placement of application, and the correct sanitary and safety procedures. Things like wrapping a client's hairline in cotton. Basically, you bring big containers full of Cholesterol—a inexpensive conditioner you can get at beauty supply stores—and gel. You take different sections of hair and do a 'relaxer retouch,' a 'root retouch,' a 'full head.' By the end, your whole station is a mess, you're a mess, you throw everything into a trash bag and leave."

Once again, he received his results in less than a week—he passed. To get a copy of your license, you have to order it off the website, for $30. If you work at two different locations, you have to display it at each. You renew it every few years by going online and paying a $20 registration fee.

LICENSING BOARDS ARE ENORMOUS bureaucracies that move at the pace of sand, and therefore tend to be very behind the times in terms of fashion trends. Recall Vidal Sassoon's outrage in 1965 over being told that if he wanted to cut hair in New York City he had to pass an exam proving that he could do finger waves and reverse pin curls—styles that women hadn't worn in decades. Because beauty schools teach directly to the exam, they, too, are often behind the times.

These days, though braiding has become a very popular

style among African Americans, the skill is only touched on in beauty school, and not given enough time. As LeMoine puts it, "Beauty school is essentially about passing the sanitation test. You learn how to cut hair, but you don't learn enough about how to work with all the various textures."

Because of this, many states now offer stand-alone "non-traditional" licenses for "specialty" services used exclusively for African American hair. In New York State, for instance, the Division of Licensing Services offers a Natural Hair Styling license that includes shampooing, arranging, dressing, twisting, wrapping, weaving, extending, locking, or braiding a person's hair. It does not include cutting, shaving, trimming, or the application of dyes, reactive chemicals, or other preparations to alter the color or structure of the hair.

Whereas New York includes hair braiding within the range of services provided with a Natural Hair Styling license, twenty-two states don't have any specific laws on the books at all, meaning anyone can braid someone else's hair for money. Seven states, including Colorado, Iowa, and Oregon, require braiders to complete one thousand hours of a standard cosmetology program. Ten states have specialty licenses for hair braiders—for instance, Texas—which requires thirty-five hours of education.

6

An extraordinary and underknown fact about the contemporary hair industry is that it has the best employment prospects out of all professions in the United States. According to a recent report by the Bureau of Labor Statistics, jobs for people who work with hair—that is, barbers, hairstylists, and cosmetologists—are projected to grow thirteen percent from 2016 to 2026, the fastest of all occupations. This is significantly better than the national average for all other occupations, which is seven percent.

There are two explanations for this growth. The first is plain old demographics. Over the next decade, America's population will continue to increase, and more people means more haircuts. The second explanation could be filed under "vanity," "fashion trends," or "Instagram," depending on your point of view. That is, the demand for hair coloring and hair straightening is expected to remain steady, meaning that the demand for professionals who can master these advanced hair treatments will, as well.

How much money hairstylists can expect to make varies by state and the salon's exclusivity. A job at a chain like Supercuts, for instance, pays less than a high-end boutique parlor on Madison Avenue. In May 2017, the annual mean wage of hairdressers, hairstylists, and cosmetologists was $21,750–$45,680. The top-paying state was the District of Columbia ($45,680; with an hourly mean wage of $21.96), followed by Washington state ($40,680), then Massachusetts, New Jersey, and Virginia (roughly $37,000). This is an average, meaning that quite a few hairstylists make much more than that.

It isn't all easy street, however. The Labor Department takes care to note that there will remain strong competition for jobs at higher-paying salons, of which there are relatively few, and for which applicants must complete with a large pool of experienced workers.

THE BUMBLING PROFESSOR. THE Rapacious Lawyer. The Needy Actress. There's an unflattering caricature for nearly every profession, but few are as divorced from reality as the Dumb Hairdresser.

According to this stereotype, people go to beauty school because they didn't go to college, and the only reason they didn't go to college is because they couldn't get in. Or worse, they never finished high school to begin with—like Frenchy in the 1978 musical *Grease*, who was thrown out of beauty school after "a little trouble in tinting class."

Along with being inaccurate and insulting, the stigma presents a genuine barrier to entry. More than a few hairstylists I interviewed admitted that it took them a long time to come around to considering beauty school a legitimate career path because they (or their parents) believed the false advertising, and thought the only way to be smart was to go to college.

There are several explanations for how this stigma came to be. The first is plain old misogyny. Culture has long liked to remind women that they are only as good as they look—and then shame them for caring.

A fascinating example of how deep this goes is the Renaissance painting *Triptych of Earthly Vanity and Divine Salvation*, by Hans Memling. Finished in 1485, it shows a woman with long brown hair standing in a garden wearing nothing but a headband and sandals. In her right hand she holds a mirror—a common symbol in Renaissance artworks of female vanity. But the mirror served another purpose, as well. As the art historian John Berger has explained, "You painted a naked woman because you enjoyed looking at her, you put a mirror in her hand and you called the painting *Vanity*, thus morally condemning the woman whose nakedness you had depicted for your own pleasure." By making it seem as if the woman considered herself foremost as a visual object, the painter was justified in his objectification of her.

The same goes for contemporary America. Girls are taught to invest a great deal of value in their looks, as if surface appearances are the most important thing in the world, but anything having to do with surface appearances—fashion, hair, makeup—is deemed superficial and frivolous, not "important." By extension, jobs in these so-called superficial realms—fashion stylists, hairstylists, makeup artists—are branded as nonserious and inessential. Likewise, because of America's puritanical attitudes toward sex and the body, professions that involve nurturing forms of physical contact—masseuse, nurse, yoga instructor—are coded as "feminine." Which brings us back to sexism. Historically, whatever is "women's work"—such as nursing and teaching—has lower prestige than jobs that are considered "male."

There is also the matter of class and status. Ever since the end of World War II, when the GI Bill made it possible for more people than ever before to attend college, an undergraduate degree has been considered an essential passport to economic and social advancement. One result is a certain snobbery toward those who don't go to college, and around vocational schools in general. (Note that it's not this way in Europe, where both serving food and styling hair are respected professions.)

The final explanation has to do with the narrow way in which America defines intelligence. Because our culture is besotted with scientific and technological progress, it heralds doctors, scientists, and computer programmers—those who tend to be qualitative and analytical thinkers—as what it looks like to be "smart." It is easy to see how this bias would result in the common misconception that a hairstylist is the polar opposite. In fact, hairstyling draws on a variety of types of intelligence: emotional intelligence, social intelligence, spatial awareness, technical prowess, creativity, and intuition.

WHEN LEMOINE FINISHED BEAUTY school, she applied to work at one of the Aveda salons in Minneapolis, but a teacher suggested that she contact Horst Rechelbacher himself and ask if he needed an assistant. And so she did. She called him up and said, "If you're looking for someone, I can be anywhere you need me to be on ten minutes' notice." That was that. She was hired.

She continued the pace she'd begun during beauty school: working seven days a week, fourteen hours a day, for a year. "All I did was work. I was super serious. No boyfriend. Horst asked me if I was gay all the time," LeMoine recalls.

Rechelbacher was a cutter, but he didn't do color. At that point LeMoine didn't, either, but because she was coloring her own hair all the time—various shades of red or orange, usually—and because her parents were hairdressers, Rechelbacher made her do all the color corrections.

Little did he know about LeMoine's Bad Color Job story.

It had happened toward the end of beauty school, in 1983. She'd been coloring her hair blue and pink for a while, and now she decided that she wanted it to be steel gray. Instead, it turned green. She didn't mind terribly much, but the following day her teacher needed a model in class and decided it should be her. The idea was to turn her green hair blonde. She didn't particularly like the color they wound up with, so the following day she bleached it again. The next thing she knew she was walking to class and—*poof*—a gust of wind blew all that overprocessed hair off her head. "I looked like a dandelion!" she laughs. Fortunately, her work as a cook at the restaurant didn't require that she interact with the public, so her bosses didn't mind when she walked in that evening looking like a beleaguered weed. The next day a friend shaped her remaining hair into a flat crew cut and dyed it black.

"The thing is, when I hire hairdressers, if I had a choice between a girl with beautiful lovely long hair and someone with hair jacked up to there, I'd hire the girl with the jacked-up hair. Because it says to me that she's experienced it," LeMoine says.

Another great educational moment also had to do with her untraditional hairstyles. This time it was when she was shaving lines in her head, in the shape of a big arrow. She was at school, walking through the waiting area for models, when she heard one of the models say, "Ugh, I hope she doesn't get my name. I don't want that woman with the weird hair cutting mine." As luck would have it, that's exactly what happened: LeMoine got her name. "This is when I first learned how important it is to comfort clients," she says now. "When I realized that I was scaring people, I learned that I really had to sit down with them and look them in the eye and discuss what they want to do. It's a really important skill, knowing how to instill confidence, and really listening to what they're saying."

Another "Ah-hah!" moment was when LeMoine suddenly understood that cutting hair has a lot to do with geometry. When a good stylist is cutting your hair, they're not simply getting rid of the part that's too long. They're also pulling the hair away from the head at specific angles to achieve different results. To envision this, picture pulling a lock of hair straight out from the head at a ninety-degree angle. That's the "neutral" position; cutting it will create a straight, blunt line. "Layering" is when you pull the lock up to a forty-five-degree angle or higher; cutting at this angle removes weight and bulk. "Graduation" is when you pull the hair down to below a ninety-degree angle, which preserves weight. "Overdirection" is when you take a lock of hair from the front, and pull it all the way to the back; after you cut, it will lie down softer. This is why clients sit in chairs that can be moved up and down. If someone very tall comes in, and the hairstylist is very short, she needs to be able to adjust the chair so that she can have full range over his head. One day, while working on a model's hair in class, all of this suddenly fell together for LeMoine. "I thought to myself, OK, this isn't rocket science, but I get it. I get it."

Another time, a woman came in who had psoriasis on her scalp, and her fine hair barely covered the scabs. "I knew I couldn't make her beautiful," LeMoine says, "but I also knew that if I changed the way her hair fell, and if I could talk her into getting some highlights that would make her hair color appear closer to the skin of her scalp, that it would diffuse the eye and make the scabs less visible. I couldn't make her beautiful, but I could definitely make her more beautiful than she was. You can't take someone who has fine hair and is balding and make them look like Farrah Fawcett, but you can work with what they have to make them better than they are."

She learned a great deal while working for Rechelbacher and loved every minute of it. "It was incredible to be a fly on the wall for this very eccentric, amazing hairdresser," she says. They traveled out of state together at least once a month, to various hair shows. She did all the colors for him. "It was a great experience because he'd say, 'Make her red with a little something extra.' I had total artistic freedom," she says. It was so fun, traveling and staying at five-star hotels, even if she had to carry all the baggage herself. Once, when she traveled without him, the airport clerks weighed all the luggage and she learned it was two hundred and seventy-five pounds. On that specific trip, she had to get a cabdriver to drive her and the luggage to a different terminal within the same airport.

Then there was the hair show when Rechelbacher had two models on stage with blond hair down to their waists. One wanted to cut it all off, the other didn't. He cut the wrong one. As soon as it happened, the model started crying.

Rather than deal with her himself, Horst made LeMoine take over. "Let's just say that because he was always hurting people and making them bleed or whatever, that I got really, really good at customer service," she laughs.

After a year, she was promoted to stylist. This was great news—except for the fact that the hiring director at the local Aveda network decided to station her at a salon in the suburbs of Minneapolis, instead of in the city, where LeMoine wanted to stay. After seven months she was finally able to switch to a salon downtown, where she stayed for the next several years.

In 1987, when she was twenty-four, she decided that she was ready for a change, and she and her best friend moved to Boston, Massachusetts. Back in Minnesota, the fact that she'd worked for Rechelbacher opened any door she wanted, but his name didn't carry as much weight yet on the East Coast, and it took longer than she'd anticipated to find work at a salon. Meanwhile, it was the early days of the AIDS crises, and her friend was dying of the disease. LeMoine took care of him, managing his medications and bringing him to his doctor's appointments. When she finally found a job, it wasn't a good fit. Eventually she wound up at a high-end salon on Newbury Street staffed with thirteen gay men, one gay woman, and one straight man. "They were all thirty percent better than I was," LeMoine says. "They were people I could learn from. But instead, everyone was just catty, and always putting everyone else down. I never felt good enough."

Then came an important turning point. One day, after LeMoine had finished with a client, and she was leaving the salon, her boss said, "That was a nice graduated bob." LeMoine shook her head and immediately started pointing out everything that was wrong with it, and what she could have done better. He looked at her and said, "I'm giving you a compliment. Take it." LeMoine pauses, recounting the story. "That was a huge moment for me," she says. "I realized that if I was going to make it, I had to believe that I was good." Not too long after, LeMoine's best friend died. She decided she'd had enough with Boston and moved to New York.

By now it was 1988, and Horst Rechelbacher was opening Aveda's first salon in Manhattan on Fifty-Third Street and Madison Avenue. In a blink, LeMoine dropped in right where they'd left off. "It was a comeback, a return. Because I'd worked for him, I was kind of the guardian of his thing, except this time around I wasn't a scared kid anymore. I could tell him with gusto what I actually thought." Within three weeks of moving she met the man she'd eventually marry.

In 1992, not long after her wedding, LeMoine decided she was ready to leave Aveda and try something new. A woman she knew had a salon on the Lower East Side, on Ludlow Street, and she rented a station from her. "But my customers from Madison Avenue wouldn't come down," LeMoine says. "They'd say that their husbands wouldn't let them. Ludlow Street was riddled with drugs. The Lower East Side was bad, bad, bad back then."

At the time, most salons were posh businesses on Madison Avenue. It was either that or Astor Place Hairstylists—a beloved combination barber shop-salon in a huge basement off St. Mark's Place known for its eclectic, grungey atmosphere—and nothing in-between. LeMoine needed a place that was nice enough to retain her clients, but was also something that she could afford. She didn't actually want to own a salon. She'd seen enough with her father, and all that he'd gone through to keep a small business going. But, at the same time, she couldn't find an atmosphere she liked. There were pluses and minuses everywhere she looked. Uptown was too stuffy and downtown was too dangerous. By then, she'd worked in enough good salons to know what she did and didn't want.

Meanwhile, she'd noticed that just a few blocks north of Ludlow Street, boutique shops and small restaurants were popping up in the East Village. She sensed that something was happening—that the neighborhood was beginning to grow in a new direction, and that she'd be wise to get in on the ground floor.

So in 1993, with her husband's encouragement, she rented a little space on Ninth Street and Avenue A. It was only one hundred and fifty square feet, a one-chair salon, for $950 a month. She found an Art Deco mirror at a flea market and hung it on the wall. Then she bought a second one. The moment she did, someone walked in saying that they wanted to work there. She hired her. Each time she bought one of those mirrors a new employee came along. Then, in 1996, LeMoine had her first child, a son.

By 1999 Parlor was three chairs and five hairdressers. They were busting out of the little address. "I'd always wanted to be able to pass on the knowledge I'd acquired, and I needed space to be able to hire assistants and train them," LeMoine says. That's the year she moved to her current location, on Avenue B between Sixth and Seventh Streets, just below Tompkins Square Park; she and her husband and son lived on the north side of the park.

Directly after she opened the new salon, her daughter

was born. Fortunately, her husband's work as a photographer meant he could take on the bulk of the daytime childcare, while LeMoine's schedule was just flexible enough to allow her to breast-feed. Each day she'd wake up, breast-feed her daughter, walk across the park to the salon, do two haircuts, walk back home, breast-feed again, go back to the salon. And so on.

She'd been right about the neighborhood. In 2000, *The New York Times* cited LeMoine as one of the reasons the area had "acquired a patina of affluence and stylishness even as it remains a bastion of middle-class dwellings and subsidized housing." In the article, LeMoine mentions that when she'd first moved there, "People would say, 'What, you're going to charge $50 a haircut? Do you know where you are?' Now I charge $80." (Today she commands nearly twice that amount.)

By 2009, business was going so well that she completed a full renovation of Parlor. In 2012 she opened the second location, on Atlantic Avenue between Third and Fourth Avenues, on the border of downtown Brooklyn and Clinton Hill.

Then, in 2015, she hit her first real bump in the road. Now that she was managing a staff that was double the size of what she'd gotten accustomed to, she tried to systematize and streamline her processes. It didn't work, exactly. She calls that year the Stroll-out—one by one, stylists left. "I'd never trained as a manager, or gone to business school, and when I was trying to systemize, I lost people," she says. It was a tough time. "I would've sold the place for ten bucks," she adds, mournfully.

Eventually, she stabilized the situation and found that the sweet spot for the payroll is twenty-three employees. That usually breaks down to roughly fourteen hairstylists, five people for the front desk, and four assistants. New hires are paid by the hour. When they get to the point where fifty percent of their clients are asking for them directly, the balance tips, and they move to a commission-based payment plan. All employees get full health benefits and four weeks of vacation a year.

She also has a larger team of advisers and contractors: a labor attorney, a regular attorney, a real-estate attorney, a life coach, an accountant, a bookkeeper, an architect, a designer, an illustrator, a social media expert/blogger (a former client), a cleaning person, and a handyman ("Way better than a husband!" she jokes; she's been divorced since 2006).

It's a lot to manage. To decompress, LeMoine takes her dogs to her house in upstate New York each weekend and works on her garden.

7

The following hair-industry truism came up so often in my reporting that it bears worth repeating: All good hairstylists possess a talent for working with their hands and emotional intelligence. The rest is up to personal temperament.

Looking back, LeMoine suspects that the real reason her parents didn't want her to become a hairdresser was because they simply didn't like the work very much themselves. She distinctly remembers when her father lost interest in cutting hair. He was only in his midthirties. He was good with his hands and liked talking with people—women especially. Because of that, cutting hair seemed a better fit than work that required mechanical know-how but little human interaction, like being an electrician or plumber. But because he wasn't drawn to the creative aspects of the job, when the industry changed, he didn't. The new demands being placed on hairdressers to have more sophisticated hair-cutting skills exhausted him. He just wasn't interested in keeping up with the times.

The roll-and-set method had been about making a woman's hair conform to a preexisting style, with no regard for its natural texture. It was less about cutting hair and more about shaping it with combs, rollers, and hair spray. Thin, flat, straight hair could be teased with a fine-toothed comb until it stood on end, and then molded into a poufy bouffant that stayed in place with the help of liberal amounts of bobby pins and aerosol hairspray. Thick, curly hair could be brushed into submission. At the end of the day, no matter what a person's hair was like naturally, everyone looked more or less the same.

Vidal Sassoon had liberated women from this high-maintenance lifestyle. In the 1960s and 70s, he paid close attention to *how* a person's hair grew from her head and introduced a method of holding up sections of hair at an angle so that when cut, it fell in a certain way, whether adding more body or taking some out. For the first time in history, a haircut was meant to work *with* a person's hair instead of against it, and as such they no longer needed elaborate roll-and-set methods to feel like they looked good. As more and more women entered the workforce, it was simply more convenient to only have to visit the salon every four to six weeks to get a trim, and wash it at home themselves between appointments.

———

THESE DAYS, ONCE YOU'VE earned your hairstyling license, the sky is the limit. Many, like LeMoine, start out as salon stylists and go on to establish their own salons. But there are many ways to go about doing this, and a world of options beyond the salon, as well. Here are a few examples.

IF YOU MET ALAN Tosler out at a bar, or at a friend's backyard barbecue, you'd likely assume he is anything but a hairstylist. With his bright blue eyes, thick black-framed glasses, and friendly manner, the married father of two could easily be a writer who works from home, the dad most likely to chaperone school field trips. Then again, his stylishly disheveled casual attire—he's most often found in an untucked button-down or black T-shirt, slouchy jeans, and running shoes—wouldn't be out of place at a tech startup. Then he speaks, and hearing his British accent you change your mind yet again: Maybe he's a vintage racecar driver? (Indeed, he is, in his off-hours.)

IN FACT, TOSLER CO-OWNS one of the most popular salons in lower Manhattan, called Tosler-Davis. Ten floors above Fifth Avenue, just off Union Square, the bright airy loft attracts a busy mix of art-world types, media makers, and corner-office executives. If you could only hear the conversations, they'd surely be interesting.

Tosler grew up in England, which follows the apprenticeship system. Straight out of high school, and shortly before he turned sixteen, he landed an apprenticeship at Vidal Sassoon's flagship salon in the Mayfair district of London. At eighteen, he was promoted to stylist. At twenty-one, eager to see more of the world, he moved to San Francisco, where his apprenticeship papers qualified him to take the license exam. For the next five years, he traveled between salons in California and the UK before finally checking out New York City. It was while working at the now defunct Jason Croy salon that he befriended a coworker, Sean Davis, who specializes in color. In 1999, Tosler-Davis opened for business.

Nineteen years later, the duo has twenty-six employees on the payroll, including eighteen stylists and five assistants, who train for two to three years before taking on their own clients. "Beauty school just gets you the license to operate, but it doesn't have much bearing on the day to day," Tosler explains.

All of his employees start out getting a salary and benefits. Once they are promoted and start taking on their own clients, they move to the commission system. Stylists at his salon make anywhere from $100k per year to $250k per year, depending on how hard they want to work.

Pro Tip #1: "When you're starting out, find work at a salon that offers training and classes to its employees."

Pro Tip #2: "When a client is going through tough times financially, don't offer a discount on the service you're providing. Instead, just give it to them for free. This builds loyalty, and when their luck improves, and they can pay full price again, they will. Once you offer a reduced price you can never turn around and return to the higher price you'd charged before."

JEN SANTO DOMINGO LIVES in San Diego, California, but these days the easiest way to find her is to look her up on Instagram. It's here that she's drawn a cult following for her signature "French girl haircut," so-called for the beauty icons who inspired it, Jane Birkin and Brigitte Bardot. Using scissors and multiple kinds of razors to "carve" the hair, Domingo has mastered a modern take on the 1970s shag, a combination of long layers, sexy bangs—long or not, depending—and short, feathery wisps that frame the face. "It's really mindful cutting, really intuitive," she says. "I have to pay attention to how the hair is bending to get it to flip where I want it to go."

The whole point of the haircut is freedom. By playing to the natural texture and weight of the hair, Domingo's thinking goes, the client should be able to wake up, shake her head, and walk out the door looking great as she is, without having to bother with lots of styling tools and products. (This isn't to say Domingo is *anti*-product. But she is resolutely only in favor of products that are nontoxic.) That is, true effortlessness, not the kind that just looks effortless. It works on any kind of hair—straight, thick, curly, coiled, wavy, coarse, or fine.

Domingo's mode of business is just as au courant as her liberated aesthetic: for the past two years, she's been on the frontlines of the "pop-up" hairstyling vanguard. For two or three days at a time, she'll rent a station at a salon in some far-flung locale—usually Los Angeles, New York City, Portland, Oregon, or Seattle. Clients find out via old-school word of mouth, social media, and mass emails. The rest of the time she works out of her private salon in San Diego; clients book appointments through the Squarespace link on her Instagram profile.

She didn't always work this way. When she was nineteen, Domingo enrolled in the Academy of Hair Design in San Diego, California, but dropped out after getting pregnant. In her early years as a mother, she worked as a freelance makeup artist. At age twenty-eight she returned to beauty school for the second time, this time at Glen Dow Academy in Spokane, Washington, then immediately started a two-year apprenticeship at VAIN salon in Seattle. She loved it so much that she stayed for nine years. "It was the most supportive family-like environment I'd ever experienced. No competition. Never catty," she recalls.

Four years ago, when her son was old enough to leave home, Domingo decided it was time she made a change, as well. Though she was incredibly busy at VAIN, working five days a week, with triple bookings throughout the day, she felt that she'd become complacent and wasn't challenging herself anymore. "I knew I wanted something different, but I wasn't sure what that looked like," she says.

Eventually she opted to return to her native California and take some time out to slow down, surf, and take stock of what she wanted, with just a little haircutting on the side. Little did she know how slow slow could be. "I didn't realize how hard it would be to build a clientele in a new city," she said. "It was a real eye-opener."

After almost a year of depression, trying to figure out what she wanted and how she'd move forward, she contacted a woman she followed on Instagram named Jayne Matthews. She was mutual friends with Domingo's mentors and had studied at VAIN. "I had been tripping out over the degrees to which we knew the same people. Something about her aesthetic felt like I was looking at myself," Domingo says.

She booked an appointment with Matthews, who was doing a pop-up in Los Angeles. At first Domingo didn't admit that she was also a hairstylist, she just told her what she liked. But as soon as she started talking, the worlds just tumbled out: "I said, 'I'm a failing hairstylist right now. I want to know how you're doing this stuff on Instagram.' I didn't know about Instagram before, I didn't have to. I feel like a dinosaur, that I'm going to get washed away. What is the trick to this?"

Matthews was all too happy to help. She shared everything she'd learned about social media through taking a course, and told Domingo exactly what she was doing, how many times a day she posted, and what kind of content people want to see. That day, when Domingo was leaving, she said that if Matthews ever needed assistance that she'd do it for free. And that's what she did. Domingo kept showing up to help, and Matthews kept giving her more information, which Domingo started implementing herself. Within a short time, Domingo went from 200 followers to 500. Just a year later, that number is already more than 6,000 and growing.

Pro Tip #1: "When you feel like giving up, don't."

Pro Tip #2: "Get an apprenticeship out of beauty school.

Put in all the time, effort, and energy to learning about hair that you can. It will feel impossible, but it will pay off."

TIPPI SHORTER IS A celebrity stylist. That is, she's styled the likes of Rihanna, Lady Gaga, Jennifer Hudson, and Alicia Keyes—and in so doing she's become a celebrity herself. She was the first African American spokesperson for Pantene and the global artistic director for textured hair at Aveda. Now she serves as president of the hair extension company Her Imports, which gives her the flexibility to hop on an airplane at a moment's notice to go style a celebrity's hair. As *USA Today* put it, "Shorter wears many hats—or, as she says it, 'many hairstyles.'"

Nobody is more surprised by this turn of events than Shorter herself. Growing up in Orange Beach, California, she had no idea what she wanted to do with her life. After graduating high school in 1991, she enrolled in junior college to pursue criminal justice. It didn't go well. "In fact, it was terrible," she remembers. "I wasn't focused, I didn't study, I wasn't passionate about anything."

A good friend who assisted celebrity hairstylist Jamika Wilson got pregnant and suggested that Shorter take over during her maternity leave.

Shorter was more than intrigued by the idea. She'd always loved the beauty industry. Growing up in Southern California, she was surrounded by people in show business— actors, models, entertainment executives. She herself was in a singing group. Whenever the group performed, or had photo shoots to publicize their shows, she'd volunteer to do everyone's hair and makeup. "I was probably way more passionate and talented at that than I was at singing," she laughs.

But until her friend suggested she take over her job, she'd never tuned into the fact that doing hair was a viable profession. Too many people had told her there just wasn't enough money in it. Now that she knew traditional college wasn't for her, she jumped. "I had eight months to get it together before my friend's baby was born," she says.

Shorter was smart and hardworking enough to turn a great opportunity into the first step of an amazing career.

In 1992, she enrolled in Bell Flower Cosmetology School (which no longer exists). She did it all—day school, night school, advanced classes for extra credit. Eight months later, she graduated and took over the job as Wilson's assistant in Carson, California.

Wilson turned out to be an excellent mentor, who encouraged her employees to challenge themselves. After Shorter had been her assistant for a year, Wilson pushed her to start taking her own appointments. "I was petrified," Shorter remembers. But she rose to the challenge and spent another year at the salon, building her own client base.

In 1995, Shorter decided to move to New York City. At first she lived with a friend and his mother. "She was so wonderful and kind and told me there'd be food on the table, and a roof over my head, so I didn't have to rush out and take whatever job I could find," she says. Soon enough, through a newspaper listing in the *Village Voice*, she was hired as a receptionist at a small, beautiful salon in lower Manhattan, called Devachan, which was known for its expertise in curly hair. Little did she know that her boss, Lorraine Massey, was at the time developing a hair product that would revolutionize the industry: DevaCurl. "I was literally in her kitchen boiling products, and then a decade later I saw her at a beauty show," Shorter says.

Shorter loved being at the salon, but because it was so small there wasn't room for her to grow. After six months, a young woman she'd known in California, who was now a receptionist at Crown & Glory salon in Manhattan, connected Shorter with the owner, and she became an assistant there. Within three months she was on the floor, styling hair.

In what was quickly becoming characteristic Shorter fashion, she didn't content herself with merely sitting back and slowly building a client base. Instead, she capitalized on every opportunity she could find, and when she couldn't find one, she created it herself. "Even if an opportunity wasn't *mine*," she says, "I'd think to myself, How can I make that work for me?"

By now Shorter was living with a roommate, who worked as an intern in the mailroom of a media company that published magazines. Shorter had business cards made and every morning she'd style her roommate's hair, a different style one day to the next, so that the people who worked in the media company would start noticing her. When they invariably did, and asked where she'd gotten her hair done, she'd give them Shorter's business card. In no time, employees at the magazines were Shorter's clients.

That bit of genius paved the way for Shorter's big break: *Rikki Lake*. They were doing makeovers and looking for someone who specialized in so-called "ethnic" hair. When the producers called *Essence* magazine in search of recommendations, the woman who answered the phone happened to be Shorter's client, and recommended her.

And so it came to pass that within six months of living in New York City, and at only twenty-three years old, Shorter was doing makeovers on national television. The day the segment aired, the phone at her salon lit up with calls from people hoping to book appointments with the young stylist they'd seen on TV.

After that, things moved quickly. Her very first editorial photo shoot was in 1997, for *Essence*. "The picture was probably the size of a quarter, but I didn't care, because my name was next to it, in a national magazine!" she says. Over the next several years she became the go-to hair person for magazines like *People* and *InStyle*, and moved to an Aveda concept salon known as a hot spot for anyone with textured hair (Lauren Hill, Lenny Kravitz, and even the Nobel Prize–winning novelist Toni Morrison all went there). Soon enough, she'd found her niche: textured hair with curls and coils.

In 2003, after Shorter had opened her own salon, a beautiful young singer who was just starting out booked an appointment—and changed Shorter's life. Her name was Rihanna, and she was looking for a team of people to accompany her on her rise to fame. "I'd never even been outside the United States," Shorter says. "So I got my passport, and started traveling internationally."

It was while she was working with Rihanna, whose star was rising, that Pantene tapped Shorter to become the face of a new line of hair products for women of color. She did that for ten years, until 2012, when Aveda hired her to fill a brand-new role: the global artistic director for textured hair. For five years she created classes for Aveda and represented textured hair on all of their platforms.

Shorter's newest initiative is the Textpert Collective, an education network to help diversify salon spaces and normalize textured hairstyling as an industry staple. They travel for one-on-one and salon-immersion classes, and will soon be selling brushes and combs designed specifically for textured hair.

Pro Tip #1: "It is time to banish the term 'ethnic hair.' It's not 'ethnic,' or even 'curly.' It's 'textured,' and all textures are different. You can't treat waves, curls, and coils as if they're exactly the same."

Pro Tip #2: "Tune into your natural ability. I had zero idea what I wanted to do in high school because I wasn't doing that."

FOR JAKE DAVIS, THERE is no such thing as a typical workday. Or rather, a typical workday might start at a hotel to do an early morning photo shoot with a fashion influencer, before heading over to his workplace, John Frieda Salon, in London, where clients range from regular working women to British royalty.

Davis grew up in Dublin, Ireland, and at age fifteen started working Saturdays at a local salon. When he told his parents that he wanted to do a hair apprenticeship instead of go to college, they fought with him, but when he was still wanting it a year later they succumbed, and he was hired on at Vidal Sassoon.

Over the next decade he worked in a lot of different commercial salons, places that aren't high-end or low-end, but somewhere in between. It was hard to survive in London, though. In his late twenties, when he learned that the famous hairdresser Nicky Clarke was charging £500 for a haircut, he was fascinated. How could this be?

He realized that if he wanted to make more money as a hairstylist, he'd have to go to Mayfair, where all the high-end salons are. When he showed up at Michael Van Clarke, and showed them his book, they told him he'd have to start again at the training level. "I obviously knew how to cut hair. But they have a specific technique that involves working with diamond sections around the circumference of the head, and if I wanted to work there I had to learn their ways," he says. He likens his seven years there to going to Savile Row to learn how to clip fabric or cloth.

He's been with John Frieda for the past sixteen years. His job includes not only salon styling and photos shoots, but also traveling abroad on behalf of the brand, and appearing on TV networks like QVC to talk about new products.

Pro Tip #1: "If a client is horrible to you, or just very unpleasant, the best way to handle them is to simply be nice. Not facetious, or sickly sweet. Just nice. And then, if that doesn't work, say, 'It doesn't seem that this is really working. Let me get someone else who can make you happy.' It's OK to step away."

Pro Tip #2: "I recommend not charging more than £150 for a haircut. That's what I do. It's expensive, but not super expensive, so I'm still able to attract a youngish clientele. When you start charging a lot more than that, you're mostly working with super-wealthy women who like a certain type of hair. I like being more variable."

———

LIKE EVERY HAIRSTYLIST I'VE ever met, and certainly all of those I interviewed for this book, LeMoine totally defies the stereotype of the "dumb hairdresser." Though it was her creativity that drew her to the profession, it was her great business sense that enabled her to thrive on her own terms. Now firmly established as a leader in her industry, she is squarely within what psychologist Erik Erikson called the "generative" stage of her life and career.

Erikson famously theorized that humans go through eight stages of psychosocial development. Each stage is a conflict between two warring forces. Because we are born as helpless beings into a threatening world, our initial order of business as infants is to develop basic trust in a caretaker who will attend to our needs. This stage, stage one, is known as Trust vs. Mistrust.

Stage seven, ages forty to sixty-five, is known as Generativity vs. Stagnation. By now, we have more or less settled into our personal lives, whether that means marriage, a long-term partnership, or a satisfying singledom. Many are experiencing the pleasures (and demands) of raising children. Our careers are more or less established, and we're either making progress in our chosen profession or questioning whether this is what we want to keep doing for the rest of our lives.

This is when things get interesting. Erikson believed that, if we're lucky, during this stage we learn that "giving back" to the world—whether being a parent or otherwise mentoring the next generation—provides us with an additional sense of purpose and makes our lives feel more meaningful.

LeMoine is among the lucky ones. Twenty-five years ago she risked her savings to open Parlor, and now it's a wildly popular two-location salon. She isn't merely progressing in her career—she's an established leader in her industry. A single mother to two grown children, with an apartment in the city and a weekend house upstate, she not only single-handedly oversees the operations of a complicated business but is responsible for the livelihoods of more than twenty employees, all of whom—and this is, right now, the most crucial detail—she generously mentors. She could be a walking advertisement for Erikson's theory that "giving back" is an excellent way to create meaning and contentment at midlife.

As she put it: "All those years I was building my own skills, my own business. Now I see myself as someone who is molding and growing hairdressers. It's really nice that this is a craft that you can pass on to people."

8

I t is another sweltering August morning, and LeMoine is wearing a long black skirt and a black T-shirt with the words *KARMA DHARMA*. It is Monday, Class-Cutting Day at Parlor.

LeMoine has always been deeply invested in education, for herself and her employees. "One of the great pleasures of this job is that there's always something new to learn," she says. It is important to her that she and her employees know how to do all types of hair. She attends classes both to keep her own skills fresh, and to provide them to her employees. Every Monday morning, the East Village location is closed to the public for Parlor Education Day, an intensive hands-on workshop in which assistants practice different hairstyles on mannequin heads, and then, in the afternoon, provide discount cuts and services.

As the assistants settle in, LeMoine bustles about, putting Styrofoam heads on stands and donning each one with a synthetic wig. Wigs made of plastic hair go for about $20, while wigs with real hair start at $60. She buys about thirty a year—Pivot Point, out of the Chicago, has the best—all of which arrive with dark hair that is then given a new color for the first lesson. After that, each wig undergoes about four haircuts. At Halloween, she sets out a big box of used-up wigs on the sidewalk for people to take. Mannequin hair is actually more difficult to cut than real hair, as it comes out of the "head" differently than it would in real life. But it's financially unreasonable to only practice on real hair. Finally, she carries a mannequin head with a long, straight, blonde wig to an out-of-the-way spot by the window. She's already blow-dried it silky-smooth, and now she starts brushing it out in long, gentle strokes. The blonde hair glimmers.

Once everyone has taken their seats, Bryzow hands out a two-page worksheet. Bryzow is a senior stylist. These days her brown hair is streaked with platinum, and cut into short baby bangs that frame her eyeglasses and face; she has a piercing in each cheek, and her lips are painted bright red. Her arms, bare in a sleeveless turquoise sundress, are covered in tattoos (including a pair of scissors, a hairstyling classic). In each ear she wears a tiny silver stud earring of a hand giving the middle finger.

Today she is teaching Jasmine, Hannah, and Alysia, all in their early twenties.

For this lesson, the stylists are revisiting material they learned in beauty school about the basic principles of haircutting—lines and angles. Before class, they each looked through magazines and on the internet for a photograph of a haircut to replicate. The worksheet is a game plan that breaks down how the stylist will approach the cut. Typed across the first page in bolded letters is the question, "How would I create this haircut?" Beneath it are three sections:

SHAPE
What is the shape of the perimeter?
What is the shape of the interior?

WEIGHT
Where is the weight built?
Where is the weight removed?

MOVEMENT
Is there a flow in a certain direction?

THE FOURTH SECTION, ON the second page, is called PLAN. Underneath is the question "What techniques are used (one length, graduation, layering)?" Below that is a line drawing of a woman's bald head seen from three different angles: the front, the side, and the top. Each assistant will draw a map of sorts over this illustration, showing what their haircut will look like. In time, these steps will become intuitive, but early on they must be spelled out and broken down.

Jasmine holds up a photo on her iPhone of a woman in a soft pixie cut.

Hannah holds up a page of *Elle* magazine showing two short pixie cuts.

Alysia has also chosen a short cut, though the one she's interested in is more of a long bob with layers.

"Would that bob challenge you?" Bryzow asks.

"A pixie cut would challenge me more, but this one seems more realistic, more like something someone would ask for," Alysia says.

"Pixies are pretty common, actually," Bryzow says, then moves on to the next person, saying to the group, "This exercise is about planning a haircut, not about having one that will be in your repertoire."

In the meantime, Hannah has decided that of the two cuts she'd chosen that she'll go with the one that Kris Jenner is wearing.

Bryzow looks closely at the style. "Remember: shape is created by weight and movement," she says. "Where the weight is preserved, and where it flows, is what determines the shape. The perimeter is the bottom of the haircut. The interior is whatever is within. For instance, you might have an A-line perimeter with layers within."

At 11:25 a.m. everyone fills out the worksheets.

Jasmine speaks up. "I can't see the back of the head in this photo."

"That's OK," says Bryzow. "You can imagine whatever you want."

"I could do a point," Jasmine decides.

"Is the perimeter of a pixie round?" Hannah asks.

Bryzow says that it is, and tells the group to just write down their first instincts, and they'll discuss them afterward. She reminds them that one haircut can have three different things going on, one at the nape of the neck, one at the back/sides, and one at the top.

By 11:30 a.m., Bryzow realizes that nobody really knows how to draw the haircuts. "It's just a way of communicating which technique you're using in what section. You're giving an overall idea," she says.

Bryzow is very good at explaining the lesson plan and, being patient, it's clear she's the child of academics. "Remember, when you pull hair backward when you cut it, it creates a forward flow," she says to the room in general. While she talks, she walks around, checking on progress. "What I want to see is what the haircut would look like if it was blown into space, 3D, like an aerial view. Not just a *picture* of the haircut."

By now LeMoine has finished brushing out the mannequin's long, blonde hair and is snipping the ends very lightly. She holds the scissors so the points are straight up and at an angle.

Jasmine completes her worksheets first and, once everyone else has finished, she is put in the hot seat. She holds up her iPhone with the photo of the pixie cut. Then she holds up her drawing. "The front will be round, and the back will be pointed in a V," she says. "The interior has graduation on the sides."

Bryzow stresses that the sides will be *very graduated*.

Next up is Alysia. She holds up her iPhone so everyone can see the cut she's chosen: it's half-pixie, half-bob.

Though to the untrained eye they all chose cuts that look almost more or less the same, in fact each one presents a different set of methods, techniques, and approaches. Each section of hair needs to be held out from the head at a specific angle and then connected to the sections on either side of it, which is its own unique challenge. There is much to consider when approaching a haircut: the texture of the hair, how it grows from the head, the shape of the head, and how much time it will take.

Bryzow studies Alysia's worksheet and says, "Go ahead and do it this way, following your instincts, so you can see cause and effect. Afterward I'll show you how I would have done it."

When it's Hannah's turn, she holds up the photo of Kris Jenner. Bryzow notes that the square layering will preserve the corners and grabs a head to show what she means. She talks about angles, geometry.

LeMoine, who has been mostly silent so far, says, "You're a fucking genius, Bryzow! I never could have explained that."

Bryzow laughs. "Geometry was my favorite subject!"

Then LeMoine explains "meno hair"—what happens to women's hair after they go through menopause, how the hair grows differently, and becomes weaker.

At 12:30 p.m. everyone moves to their assigned mannequin. First, they wet the heads and brush out the hair, so it's ready to cut.

"Remember to keep the hair evenly saturated throughout," Bryzow says. "Having some parts that are dryer than others messes with the balance and tension."

The apprentices are very quiet and focused as they cut. She walks around from one head to the next, observing and asking questions.

LIKE SO MANY STYLISTS, when she was a child, Bryzow loved to play with hair—dolls, Barbies, she even gave her teddy bears haircuts. But she never knew it could be an actual career.

When she got to high school, a friend convinced her to join the after-school theater club and she decided to sign up for the backstage crew. "The hair and makeup team called me, and it was kismet," she says. "Two years in, and I knew I wanted it as my career. I stuck with it all four years."

Her parents are both academics—her mother is a genetic researcher and her father is a chemical engineer—and they wanted her to go to college. So she decided to study theater design and production at the University of Evansville. For the next four years, she made costumes and scenery, took literature and directing classes and learned how to work with wigs. She did the haircuts for all the shows. A lot of the time she just looked up stuff on YouTube and taught herself.

During the summer, she got a job at a theater festival making wigs. After graduating, she spent a year in Arizona making costumes, then moved to New York City in 2015, just for fun. She wound up enrolling at the Aveda Institute not long after she arrived. By the following summer she was at Parlor, where she's now been for two years.

UNLIKE MOST, SHE WASN'T daunted by the requirements of beauty school. "Math, science, safety, sanitation, geometry, design, chemistry—so much chemistry goes into hair coloring—I was into all of it. Thanks to my parents being scientists, I'm a compulsive researcher, a huge nerd," she laughs.

As the apprentices cut and chat, LeMoine and Bryzow stand to the side, observing, occasionally stepping in with advice, even brandishing their own scissors and taking a few choice snips. The hair that falls to the floor is eventually swept into piles that vanish into a stationary, touchless Eye-Vac.

Then they both step back and join me where I'm leaning against the wall. We launch into a discussion about what makes for a great hairstylist. I mention that people tend to assume that all hairstylists are extremely extroverted.

"Actually, it really varies," Bryzow says. "A lot of stylists can be really talkative one on one, but not necessarily in groups."

"There's also the matter of talking all day long at work and when you get home, you just want to be quiet," LeMoine says. "I'm like that, and my dad definitely was, too. After talking all day at the salon, he'd come home and work on the sailboat he'd made, just quietly working with his hands."

"Yeah, it's such an outward-facing job," says Bryzow. "There's a big distinction between genuine interaction and a friendly facade."

LeMoine pauses. "It's interesting. The salon space today is so similar to what it was like back when my father was working. But back then, when women came in once a week, the relationship was much more personal. Now that people come less frequently, the conversations are more about work, what trips are coming up, stuff like that. It's still personal and nice, but it's different."

Hairstyling is obviously a very personal interaction. Possibly the only person to scrutinize our reflections as closely as we do ourselves is our hairstylist, who is analyzing our features and complexions to decide which cut or color might work best. Not only that, the stylist is given free range to touch our head and scalp—an area of the body that is most commonly reserved for lovers, whether they be stroking our hair with fondness or grasping it in the throes of passion. Meanwhile, hairstylist and client often carry on a conversation that can feel—and often is—very intimate. If you stick with the same stylist over time, you can develop a sense of attachment and fondness that feels a lot like friendship.

But it's not friendship, exactly. There's a reason hairstylists are so often compared to therapists—more likely than not, it's a one-way conversation about the client's life, and not necessarily a two-way exchange. Good stylists are extremely mindful of this boundary, taking care to never cross it.

I mention a study I'd read that showed thirty-nine percent of women consider their hairdresser a friend, "someone they can talk to about personal things." Another study showed that fifty-two percent of stylists encourage clients to talk about their personal problems, but only seven percent talk about their own problems in return. Researchers call this "emotion work": managing their emotions to meet their clients' desires. In this way hairstyling is not unlike waiting tables, or being a flight attendant.

LeMoine nods yes. "If you're actual friends with your stylist—if you get together after work, or on the weekends—you either knew her before she began cutting your hair or you were the one to make the first move," she says. "The client is free to cross the line and the stylist may reciprocate. But it never goes the other way around. Not with the very good ones, at least."

They muse for a bit on the younger stylists, noting that Jasmine tends to be quiet when she cuts, while Alysia is chatty, but in a good way.

"I will say that it bothers me when they talk to clients at the shampoo station," LeMoine admits. "That should be a time for the client to be relaxing with her own thoughts."

We fall quiet, watching the assistants toil over their mannequin heads.

LeMoine breaks the silence. "Empathy is huge," she says. "Intuition. You need to be able to read between the lines and guide the conversation. I do a lot of consultation work with the apprentices. I'll point out that they didn't pay attention when the client said something—they glossed right over it."

"Also, spatial awareness," Bryzow adds. "You have to be able to see the whole haircut. A lot of brilliant art students would be great hairdressers, they just don't know it."

"You need to develop your eye so you can see right away

when something isn't right," LeMoine adds. "You have to be able to see what's wrong and find a solution."

She ponders for a moment. "People say this is a right brain industry, but really it's equal parts right brain and left brain. The left is what gives structure and longevity to the haircut."

Left brain-right brain theory is the idea that each half of the brain is responsible for different mental functions. People who are considered "left brain dominant" are quantitative, logical, and analytical, while those who are "right brain dominant" are emotional, intuitive, and creative. Though the theory is a radical simplification of what's actually going on in the brain, which is far more complicated and interconnected, it's a useful shorthand for thinking about our own tendencies and approaches to solving problems.

The conversation moves on to gender. Bryzow points out that though hairstylists are overwhelmingly women, most high-end, elite stylists are men. Not only that, on average male stylists make more money than their female counterparts. "Maybe men feel they can charge more," she theorizes.

LeMoine chimes in. "In my experience, female hairdressers take time to find out what I want. Men don't know what it's like to have hair the way women do, and they feel more free to do what they want with it."

Jasmine finishes cutting her mannequin first, then blow-dries the hair. While the rest continue working, she tells me a bit of her story.

Jasmine is twenty-four, and wears her African American hair naturally, in a bob of curls that frames her face. She wears a navy sleeveless blouse with a silver studded collar, dark blue jeans, and brown Birkenstocks. She's been at Parlor a little over a year.

Growing up, she knew she wanted to do hair, but her family wanted her to go to college, and so she studied communications technology at York College in Queens. As soon as she could, she looked up "best hair schools" on the internet and wound up at the Aveda Institute in Manhattan.

"Beauty school was a lot different than I thought it would be," she says. "When I started out, I didn't think about the math and science aspects. I was surprised by how much anatomy and geometry is involved in cutting hair. We learned the warning signs of different scalp conditions."

She met LeMoine at a career fair at her school. When she came to visit Parlor, she immediately noted how different it was from most salon environments. "It felt really down-to-earth here. Most salons make clients feel uncomfortable, like they don't know anything. That's not at all what it's like here."

She works five days a week, eight to nine hours a day. She lives in the Bronx.

"My dream is to be a really successful hairstylist and to keep learning and accepting new information as I get older," she says. "My biggest fear is shutting off from learning new things."

At 3:15 p.m., the real-life models arrive.

By 5:00 p.m., Jasmine is yet again the first to finish. The other two are still going.

Jasmine was smart to choose Parlor out of all the places to work in New York City. Between the Monday classes and LeMoine's attentive mentorship, she's sure to find what she's looking for here—the chance to continually be learning, from someone who knows in her bones the value of always accepting new information, no matter your age or life stage. Technically speaking, hairstyling is a career, but for those who are creative, always curious, always open, it's also a calling.

ACKNOWLEDGMENTS

Thank you to all the hairstylists who spoke to me for this book, illuminating the world of hair, but particularly to Gwenn LeMoine, who was so generous with her time, contacts, and knowledge. Thanks also to Karyn Marcus for her smart guidance, Carly Sommerstein and Isolde Sauer for their great fixes, and Gillian MacKenzie for her friendship.

FURTHER READING

The following books provide various perspectives on the world of hair, including science, history, and social criticism.

In the Hair: A Fashion Hairstylist's Journey of Creativity
(CreateSpace Independent Publishing Platform, 2017)
By Nicolas Jurnjack
A playful, book-length conversation with a world-renowned French hairstylist about his decades-long career working with famous models and actresses around the globe.

Entanglement: The Secret Lives of Hair (Oneworld, 2016)
By Emma Tarlo
A UK anthropology professor embarks on a personal quest to understand her own fascination with hair. The result is a lively, conversational investigation of the fashion industry, and a history of the stuff that grows out of our heads.

hair (Bloomsbury, 2016)
By Scott Lowe
This tour of global hair customs written by a former philosophy and religious studies professor is quite short, but long on fascinating facts.

Hair: A Human History (Pegasus Books, 2016)
By Kurt Stenn
One of the world's leading hair follicle experts delivers an information-packed look at the biology, physiology, and history of hair. If you want to understand follicles, shafts, genes, and growth patterns, this is your book.

Milady Standard Cosmetology (Milady, 2015)
By Milady
The most commonly used resource in beauty schools across the nation, this enormous textbook teaches you everything you need to know about mastering the science and art of cosmetology.

Hair: Fashion and Fantasy (Thames & Hudson, 2013)
By Laurent Philippon
A visual feast of rare archival images and iconic photographs accompanied by witty commentary from fashion stars ranging from Vidal Sassoon to Dita Von Teese.

Hair: Styling, Culture and Fashion (Berg, 2008)
Edited by Geraldine Biddle-Perry and Sarah Cheang
This anthology of essays about the importance of hair collects a range of academic and theoretical perspectives.

Rapunzel's Daughters: What Women's Hair Tells Us About Women's Lives (Farrar, Straus and Giroux, 2004)
By Rose Weitz
Another engaging exploration of hair's public and private influences, this one by a sociologist. The chapter "At the Salon" is devoted to the profession of hairstyling.

Hair: Public, Political, Extremely Personal (St. Martin's Press, 2000)
By Diane Simon
Inspired by her own so-called "bad" hair, the author explores the racial connotations of hair in America and around the globe.

Big Hair: A Journey into the Transformation of Self (The Overlook Press, 1995)
By Grant McCracken
An insightful ethnography of women's hair and the hairstyling industry by an anthropologist of consumer culture.

ABOUT THE AUTHOR

Kate Bolick's first book, *Spinster: Making a Life of One's Own*, was a *New York Times* bestseller and a *New York Times* Notable Book of 2015. A contributing editor for the *Atlantic*, she writes for a variety of publications here and abroad, including the *New York Times*, the *Wall Street Journal*, *Cosmopolitan*, *Elle*, and *Vogue*, and hosts "Touchstones at The Mount," an annual interview series at Edith Wharton's country estate, in Lenox, MA. She teaches nonfiction writing at New York University and Columbia University, speaks frequently at colleges and conferences, and has appeared on the *Today* show, CNN, MSNBC, and numerous NPR programs across the country. Her introduction to the new Penguin Classics edition of Charlotte Perkins Gilman's collected writings is forthcoming in 2019.